The Complete Guide to Beagles

Tracey Squaire

LP Media Inc. Publishing

www.lpmedia.org

Publication Data

Tracey Squaire

The Complete Guide to Beagles---- First edition.

Summary: "Successfully raising a Beagle dog from puppy to old age" --- Provided by publisher.

ISBN: 978-1-79805-113-9

[1. Beagles --- Non-Fiction] I. Title.

This book has been written with the published intent to provide accurate and author-itative information in regard to the subject matter included. While every reasonable pre-caution has been taken in preparation of this book the author and publisher expressly dis-claim responsibility for any errors, omissions, or adverse effects arising from the use or application of the information contained inside. The techniques and suggestions are to be used at the reader's discretion and are not to be considered a substitute for professional veterinary care. If you suspect a medical problem with your dog, consult your veterinarian.

Design by Sorin Rădulescu

First paperback edition, 2019

TABLE OF CONTENTS

CHAPTER 17

Advanced Beagle Health and Aging Dog Care

CHAPTER 1
What to Know Before Choosing a Beagle

What is a Beagle?

"Beagles are the most curious little dogs. They love to please. When my mother would explain the personality of a Beagle she would simply say that they were 'Pleasers'. If they knew the person they loved wanted something they would do anything to make that loved one happy."

Jennifer Eaton Lopez
Little Beagles

Once bred as scent hounds to assist in the hunting of rabbits and other small game, Beagles are now one of the most popular dog breeds in North America. From singles in city apartments to couples in the suburbs, dog lovers of all kinds will find a Beagle to be a great choice as a furry companion. This purebred hound is popular among Americans and Canadians for its small size, fun-loving attitude, and overall-friendly nature.

Beagles are a breed full of energy which they use to track any scent their amazingly enhanced noses catch hold of, so whether it's a sprint to the store, a hike along a forest trail, or an excursion into the backyard, a Beagle will find an interesting scent to keep him running toward the next stop.

This breed might seem overly-mischievous and stubborn at first because of its high intelligence and one-track nose, but gentle-yet-firm training often presents a loyal and intelligent family companion.

Whether the Beagle is a purebred or one of the ever-more-popular Beagle mixes, Beagles remain charismatically smart, loving, and loyal dogs.

If you're thinking of adding a Beagle to your family or have already done so, it's important to learn all you can to ensure you have the knowledge to raise a healthy and happy Beagle that reflects its solid canine ancestry.

History of the Beagle

Before you add a Beagle to the story of your life, learn about the long history Beagles and humans have together.

Beagles have an interestingly mysterious history as there are many different breeds that could have possibly contributed to the lineage of the modern Beagle.

Even the word Beagle has no clear origin. The earliest mention of Beagle in English literature is from The Squire of Low Degree, a late-Middle English verse romance published in 1475. The exact origination of the word is unclear, though it could come from the French word "begueule," meaning "loud or wide mouth" (an apt description of these howlers, so be warned).

Photo Courtesy of Jamie-lee Wood

Photo Courtesy of
Bernard Williams

Other possible origins include the German word begele, meaning "to scold" (which you will do a lot of with this naughty breed) and the Celtic word beag, which just means "small," also very apt.

Regardless of where the name originated from, Beagles have an impressively charming lineage to add to the mystery of its name.

Although the breed as we know it didn't exist until the 19th century, a version of the Beagle has been around as an animal companion for over 2,500 years to ancient Greeks and European hunters.

The modern breed is descended from a mix of hounds native to Great Britain such as the now-extinct packs of nine-inch tall "Pocket Beagles" Queen Elizabeth I kept (which sounds scary and cute at the same time), but the canine ancestor thought to be mostly responsible, in part, for the Beagles we enjoy today is the St. Hubert Hound, a breed with a bloodline traced back to the seventh century. These hounds were supposedly brought to England by William the Conqueror and were used for deer hunting.

Beagles began being introduced to North America around the 1840s as hunting dogs, giving American breeders their chance to contribute to the Beagle lineage, which they did with gusto.

The Talbot hound, now extinct, was a popular hunting dog for breeders through which to herald new generations of Beagles. The Talbot holds the same status of the St. Hubert Hound as an ancestor of modern Beagles and, in fact, is from the St. Hubert line itself.

American breeders and British breeders alike worked together to ensure the fitness, the attractiveness, and more importantly, the survival of the Beagle breed, and are responsible for the companions we have today since the Beagle breed has fallen out of popularity many times in its long history.

In 1887, Beagle breeders in England had been working for some time to improve the number of Beagle packs as there were only 18 established packs at the time. Those breeders weren't willing to let this highly useful and companionable breed be forgotten to time. In 1902, The Beagle Club and The Association of Masters of Harriers and Beagles, together, brought the number of Beagle packs up to 44, a success that was a long time coming and which helped re-spark Beagle popularity.

By the mid-19th century in America, Beagles were deeply ensconced in society as show dogs, hunting dogs, and companion dogs, and they were bred specifically for all three purposes. With previous breeders being more focused on the utilitarian traits of the Beagle, breeders at this time, such as General Richard Rowett, worked to improve the appearance of the breed by importing Beagles from British breeders who had been working (successfully!) themselves to improve the attractiveness of Beagles.

American breeders went even further with importing for looks with James Kemochan, an old celebrity in the Beagle breeding community, pushing the appearance of Beagles closer to that of the hound look we know and recognize today.

While the breed's popularity temporarily dropped in England after World War I, North Americans continue to find enjoyment in Beagles today. With such a long-lasting and rich heritage and a history full of dog-show award winners, it's no surprise that the Beagle has stayed popular in North America since its introduction.

FUN FACT
The First Beagles

The first Beagle-type hunting dogs can be traced back to 400 BC Greece where they were bred to hunt hares. Around 200 AD, these small pack dogs were brought to Britain and were interbred with British hounds. The breed evolved into what we know today as Beagles around the 15th century in England, France, Italy, and Greece. The name comes from the Celtic language "beg" or "beag," meaning "small." Queen Elizabeth I was known to have a pack of beagles who were about nine inches in height. The breed prospered in Great Britain and Ireland during the 19th century. In America, General Richard Rowett bred his dogs with imported British hounds. The breed grew in popularity and reputation as a superb scent dog. Today, beagles are not only beloved family pets, but they are used in field and pack trials, for drug detection by law enforcement, termite inspection for homes, and as well-loved therapy dogs.

Physical Characteristics

"They come in many shapes, sizes and colors that range from all black to all white and literally every shade in between. I even saw a litter of Champagne pink coloration that came from a pair of smoke colored parents. There are even a few Leopard spotted Beagles. They come as small as some Toy breeds and some get big enough to rival Labradors."

Gregg Moore
Moore Beagles

The most recognizable part of a Beagle's appearance besides its large, floppy ears and adorably pleading eyes is its smooth double coat. With clear influence from the St. Hubert Hound's black and tan coat and the brilliant white coat of its Talbot ancestors, a purebred Beagle can be spotted by its white-tipped tail, which helped our hunter ancestors find their furry hunting companions among tall grass. Nowadays, the Beagle tail is more often raised and waved in anticipation of treats than it is to alert of nearby prey.

Beagles can come in a variety of common hound colors that are mixed and matched. Beagle coloring can get complicated and incredibly specific, but some common colors and combinations (with white as the common denominator) are:

- Classic tri (a solid black "saddle" outlined in brown fur)
- Shaded tri (black fur blurred into brown on the Beagle's rib cage)
- Lemon and white (a tan or "lemony" color instead of the typical brown or black)
- Blue/silver tri (a bluish-gray or silvery coat)

Since Beagles are recognized and categorized by height, their stature is also a notable characteristic of the Beagle breed. The American Kennel Club (AKC) recognizes only two varieties of Beagles:

Variety 1: hounds standing under 13 inches tall

and

Variety 2: hounds standing between 13 and 15 inches

Don't let the small size of these pups fool you. Beagles are quick and have the firmly solid build that lent their ancestors the power they needed to hunt hares and other small game. These pups are energetic, which is to be expected for their size and their original purpose, and their pleading expressions can sometimes be hard to combat when they're begging for food or attention.

Closely resembling Foxhounds in appearance, Beagles are much shorter than their canine cousins with broader heads, shorter muzzles, and shorter legs compared to their bodies, but those differences are exactly why Beagles continue to be popular dogs in cities and suburbs alike.

FUN FACT
What is a Beagle?

Both Beagle varieties are small, under 13 inches or between 13-15 inches. These small dogs are strong and solid. Beagles come in beautiful colors including tricolor and red and white among others. With big, brown, or hazel eyes, this hound is a pleasure to look at. With its delightful face and floppy, hound ears, you may lose your heart to this popular family dog. Beagles are inquisitive, cheerful dogs that require lots of attention and exercise to become wonderful family members.

Breed Behavioral Characteristics

"The most unique thing about beagles is their howl, bawl, or bay. Each beagle has a different sound. Some are high pitched while others have a deeper bay. Each dog has its own unique sound."

Chey Ballard
Rajun Cajun Kennels

Behavior is important to consider before choosing any companion. Some common behaviors Beagles exhibits include being:

- Energetic
- Friendly
- Stubborn
- Loving

- Mischievous
- Food-loving
- Curious
- Intelligent

Beagles truly are loving and sweet. They are childlike and playful, so they do well with children and make good family dogs. They've got a lot of energy in their tiny bodies, so they're active a lot. Even though Beagles truly are a great dog breed, they can also be stubborn and oftentimes, naughty.

Since Beagles ARE childlike, they easily become spoiled, and it's not always by their own doing. Their naturally pleading expressions and overall charming appearance entices one to sneak a Beagle pup an extra snack or two.

Beagles are pack animals and do not do well alone, but that just means this breed is excellent company. These dogs get attached quickly and easily, and Beagles do well with children and other pets because of their companionability and friendliness. Beware, though: their naturally-kind nature also makes them bad guard dogs.

Is a Beagle the Right Fit for You?

Before settling on a new Beagle, remember that Beagles need plenty of socialization. If you work from home, have other animals, or can just generally be with your Beagle often, then you'll be happy with a Beagle. Beagles who are left alone for too long, on the other hand, can become anxious and destructive, which isn't fun for anyone involved.

Photo Courtesy of Michelle Zfira

Remember also that Beagles are inquisitive and strong-willed, especially if they get a whiff of something that leads them on a tracking bender, and their friendliness isn't always a good thing when faced with strangers. You'll need to have a firm but kind hand when training these pups.

Another thing to consider is that though not all Beagles are loud or will howl, Beagles, in general, CAN be loud. My own Beagle never barks, and howls only when he's trying to get our cats to play with him, but these howls are still loud even though they are under-used. Be conscious of your neighbors' comfort as well as your own.

If you haven't been scared off by these stubborn, food-loving hounds yet, then good! Now, why exactly would you want to have a Beagle as part of your family?

Simply put, Beagles have had a long-standing place alongside humans for years, and there's a reason they've consistently topped the popular dog breed charts in North America for generations. These ancient hunting companions easily adapt to being caring lapdogs or energetic family dogs. They are gentle, smart, and merry, and those characteristics make them a joy to be around. Beagles will energize their owners as well as the other pets in their home.

If you're looking for a fresh breath of happiness in your life, choosing to add a Beagle to your family is a smart choice.

CHAPTER 2
Choosing a Beagle

Buying vs. Adopting

Now that you've decided a Beagle is the right breed for you, it's time to decide whether buying from a store, buying from a breeder, or adopting is the best choice for you.

Adopting a Beagle

Adoption is an excellent choice when adding a new member to your family, and the reality is that most pets at a shelter had a home and were taken from it for some reason, so adopting a Beagle gives you the opportunity to offer a much-wanted home.

You're much less likely to find a purebred Beagle up for adoption, but Beagle mixes more often than not have the same characteristics that make their purebred brothers so popular. Beagle mixes also offer benefits.

Photo Courtesy of Sunita Chaudhary

Some Popular Beagle Mixes
- The Beagador (a Beagle and Labrador)
- The Beagi (a Beagle and Corgi)
- The Puggle (a Pug and Beagle)
- The Borkie (a Beagle and Yorkshire Terrier)
- The Jack-a-Bee (a Jack Russell Terrier and Beagle)
- The Poogle (a Beagle and Poodle)

There are even more Beagle mixes in shelters, with far fewer purebred ancestors but who still maintain the Beagle lovability, so it's worth the time to check your local adoption centers before purchasing a purebred.

A big benefit of adoption is knowing your potential pet's personality before adoption. Shelter workers and pet fosterers usually record the personalities of their charges so that when potential adopters come looking for a new companion, they can find a pet that matches their lifestyle and personality.

Pets up for adoption may also already be trained, but do be aware that a dog may have been given up for adopt because of some behavioral problem. Don't be afraid to adopt because of behavior, though. Good training can bring out the best in any dog.

Cost is another factor in support of adoption. Buying

QUOTE
Buy or Adopt?

American novelist Arthur Phillips is a Beagle enthusiast. *"I am notorious for always having two beagles with me, in any and all circumstances."* Your choice of pet will affect your entire family and is a lifelong commitment. The decision to buy a puppy or adopt an older dog should not be taken lightly. Older dogs may need more time and greater patience to assimilate into the family unit.

a puppy, especially a purebred Beagle, can cost hundreds, if not thousands, of dollars. Most adoption fees don't go over $300 and are usually around $50.

Besides saving yourself quite a bit of money, you are also giving an animal a new outlook on life. You've got a lot of love to give, and shelter pets are in need of love and will reflect that love back as much as their tiny bodies are able.

The downside is that you may not have access to medical records, or your shelter dog may already have a bias against specific animals, sounds, people, or situations.

Buying a Beagle

If you're looking specifically for a purebred Beagle and want to ensure you don't get a Beagle mix, buying is much safer as you're more likely to have access to the lineage of potential pets.

Depending on where you're buying your dog from, your Beagle puppy may have already been microchipped and received all the shots and boosters it will need for the first year, saving you money in the first year by being bundled into the purchase price of your new pet. No matter where you get your puppy from, you want to make sure you have its medical records and parent history.

A pet store may sell pups, along with everything you'll need for the first few months of the puppy's life as well, so if you're a first-time pet owner, having your puppy come with all the supplies it needs to enjoy life can be a bonus, but pet-store puppies are very unlikely to have a

*Photo Courtesy of
Gregg Moore
Moore Beagles*

semblance of house-training unless an in-house trainer works with the puppies.

Some stores also include vouchers for spaying and neutering and offer discounts for any further supplies you purchase for your new pup at their store.

A pet store offers the most variety if you're not picky about the breed purity of your potential pet. These stores may have popular Beagle mixes as well as purebreds, though buying from a reputable breeder is the best option if you want a purebred Beagle and also want to ensure the ethical nature of the transaction.

Ultimately, it's your choice how you add a new member to your family. When buying, the important thing is to do your research to ensure you're dealing with an ethical and reputable seller, but dogs adopted from a shelter or obtained for free are just as lovable and trainable as those bought from a store or a breeder.

How to Find a Reputable Breeder

Finding an ethical breeder to purchase your new Beagle from is important if the health and suffering of puppies inside of puppy mills is a concern of yours. Puppy mills or unethical breeders exploit animals by breeding many dogs at a time in order to sell puppies for profit. Dogs from puppy mills often have health or behavioral issues related to unethical breeding practices that most people don't discover until long after they've brought home their puppy.

Responsible breeders do not sell to just anyone and constantly work to ensure the health and quality of the dogs they breed, and since you'll have between 10 and 13 years with your Beagle, you want those years to be filled with happiness and health from the beginning, and your dog's beginning is with a breeder.

Finding a disreputable breeder is easier than finding a reputable one, but that shouldn't deter you.

When looking for a reputable breeder, start with your veterinarian or the veterinarian you plan to use for your new Beagle. Vets deal often with the results of irresponsible breeding, so they're likely to point you in the direction of a good local breeder. Additionally, you can search for local breeders yourself by visiting a breeder's club if your area has one.

If you don't have a vet or a local breeder's club, you can search online for reputable breeds through a veterinarian-run site such as pupquest.org or the AKC's website. Most reputable breeders are registered on the AKC website.

Photo Courtesy of Nicole Burkett

Researching Breeders

"Go to a Breeder that has the Bloodline that suits you. Not all Beagles are created equal and everyone knows what they like. I like Speed and Drive therefore look at a Breeder that can provide this."

Gregory Hovey
Victory Hill Kennel

After you've gotten a few referrals for breeders, you can begin gathering as much information about them as possible. If you've found a breeder through the AKC website, you will be able to see the breeder's credentials there. If the breeder has a website, that's a great place to start, and you can end your web search with reviews of that breeder from other buyers.

On the breeder's site, you want to see lots of pictures of the dogs this breeder has helped produce (bonus if you see a happy and healthy mama as well). Many breeders talk explicitly about what their mission is with breeding such as improving temperament, intelligence, health issues, or appearance. Many passionate breeders will even post blogs on their sites to continue giving you information about the breeds they care for.

You don't want to see more than two different dog breeds being offered on a breeder's site as this is an indication of a puppy mill. Breeders prefer to focus on improving only one or two breeds at a time.

After you've researched a few breeders and have narrowed down your choices, ask to meet the breeders at their facilities so you can get a look around at the puppies and where they were born and raised. No reputable breeder will have a problem with you coming to see where they do their business, and if they do hesitate or refuse to let you go to their facility, choose a different breeder.

While at the facility, meet the parents of the puppies and check to see if the living areas are clean and spacious. Puppies from a breeder should be friendly and unafraid if they have been receiving proper socialization. If the breeder is not friendly or sociable with the puppies or refuses to let you meet the parents, you should be concerned.

Confirm that the breeder has lineage and breed documentation for their puppies. Many genetic health problems are present in the parents and grandparents of dogs, so your breeder should provide the medical records of both parents and should be well versed in the specific genetic problems common to Beagles.

A good breeder will also want to know as much about you as possible so they can be sure their puppies are going to a good home, so if the breeder is just trying to make a quick sell without asking you much about yourself, the breeder is likely not reputable

HELPFUL TIP
Cost Considerations

According to adoptapet.com, you can purchase a Beagle pup from a reputable breeder for upwards of $800-$1500, but can adopt a Beagle from a rescue center for approximately $300 to cover the costs of shots, spaying, or neutering. One such rescue organization is the Midwest Beagle Rescue (gotbeagles.org). Check online for rescue organizations near you.

Health Tests and Certifications

Whether you buy from a store, a breeder, or adopt, you should make sure your potential pet has the same medical checkups either provided by the pet's current owner or by your own vet. Though Beagles are generally healthy, they are prone to a plethora of health problems.

If you've bought from a breeder or a certain store, you should get a packet of information with your new puppy, including health history. This history should include any tests done on the puppy as well as diseases and health problems the puppy's parents may have had. It is vital that you receive health records and documentation about the parents of your potential puppy.

If you're dealing with a reputable breeder, you should be reviewing this information before actually meeting potential pups. You want to be able to check the validity of the certifications and documents presented to you. No reputable breeder should deny your review of these documents.

Ensuring you buy from a reputable breeder is not just to make sure you don't have a sick puppy; it ensures that the breeder is helping to maintain and improve the Beagle breed rather than exploiting it for money.

These certifications are important to keep in mind if you're buying a Beagle with thoughts of breeding as you will be equally responsible for the long-term health and quality of the Beagle bloodline.

Different dog breeds require different health tests. Beagles are required to have the following health tests:

- Hip evaluation
- Ophthalmologist evaluation
- Musladin-Lueke Syndrome (MLS) DNA Test

The breeder should also have documents certifying the health of the puppy's parents and verifying that the dogs are free of the following:

- eye diseases (which Beagles are prone to)
- abnormal hips
- abnormal thyroid
- abnormal heart

You can search the Orthopedic Foundation for Animal's website to check the legitimacy of all health certificates a breeder produces.

Breeder Contracts and Guarantees

Photo Courtesy of Miranda Schmitter

When you buy from a breeder, you will end up signing a contract. This contract is more than just a bill of sale, and not every breeder will include the same stipulations in their contract that another might.

Contracts often include information such as the name of the puppy's parents, their health information, their registration numbers, the puppy's registration number, the total cost paid, any promises or guarantees the breeder has made, and promises you've agreed to about the future of your pet, and just generally any other agreements made between the two of you.

This contract protects you, your new pet, and the breeder and is the breeder's way of outlining exactly what is expected of you when you purchase one of their purebred dogs. Reputable breeders are invested in a puppy's life even after it goes to a new home.

Choosing the Perfect Pup

When you've got all the responsibility out of the way, you can finally get to choosing the right Beagle puppy for you and your family.

Since you're already set on getting a Beagle, you should be prepared for the activity level of Beagles. If you're purchasing from a breeder, visit several times before making your decision so you can get a better sense of a specific Beagle's personality.

My own Beagle has high energy only when he's sniffing out food or strange scents. Otherwise, he's relaxed and likes to lounge with my cats. My household chose this specific dog not because of his breed but because of the calm aspect of his personality compared to the other dogs we were considering. We aren't a high-energy household, so we didn't want a high-energy dog who wouldn't be happy having low-energy owners.

Playfulness is another area for consideration. If you have children and other pets, you may want a more playful puppy. The pup who's cuddled up to mommy while its siblings tumble around with each other likely won't be the pup for you. Additionally, this action may indicate that the puppy is less confident and more afraid than its siblings and may have a higher possibility of separation anxiety.

Aggression isn't typically a problem in Beagles, but each individual dog has its own personality. Aggression may come from one of the puppies just naturally being assertive and dominant, but this is especially important to consider if you have other pets or small children. An aggressive puppy will become a harder-to-handle aggressive dog. To check for aggression, gently roll a puppy on his back and hold him in that position for a moment. If he calms down and doesn't struggle for long, he's less likely to be aggressive. Dogs who continue to struggle are more likely to be aggressive.

Not every Beagle breeder will breed the same type of Beagle, so choosing a bloodline that produces the characteristics you're looking for in a Beagle is smart. If you're looking to breed your Beagle down the line, look for a bloodline with few health problems. Communicate with the seller as much as possible. They should know their pups and should be able to give you an idea about which puppy is compatible with your lifestyle.

Tips for Adopting a Beagle

"If you are getting your Beagle from a rescue organization try to get as much back-ground on the Beagles former circumstances as you can. The Beagle may be aloof, timid or shy but should never be aggressive."

Cindy Williams
Honey Pot Hounds

If adoption is the path you choose when adding a new member to your family, you want to be more active about analyzing and choosing a new dog. Even if you're adopting, you should try to make multiple trips to see a potential pup before taking it home.

You want to gauge the personality and behavior of your potential dog right off the bat. Communicate with the shelter workers about your interests as they have insights into the personality and demeanor of the animals in their shelter. Shelter dogs are sometimes older and al-

Photo Courtesy of Amber Wheaton

ready have an established personality, but that personality may be harder to gauge if the dog is uncomfortable in the shelter setting or around strangers.

Watch the dog in his kennel before approaching him. You may need to use a kennel yourself, so if the pup is anxiously trying to claw his way out of the kennel, truly think about if you're able to handle an easily-stressed Beagle. They yelp and claw and howl, especially when they are anxious, and Beagles can be incredibly loud.

Sit with a dog for a bit so he can get used to you, then he will relax and start to show you who he is. Compare the dog's behavior with your own behavior and that of the current pets in your home. Compatibility is key with adoption.

Get as much information as you can about the dog's background as possible. Has he lived with other pets before? Children? Was he a stray or a pet given up for adoption? Many dogs are given up for adoption for behavioral problems the previous owner couldn't handle.

Common reasons a Beagle may be in a shelter:
- Runs away a lot
- Howls/barks (especially when alone)
- Bad behavior (not coming when calling, digging, escaping)

These reasons are commonly a result of the previous owner not properly training the Beagle. Beagles are smart dogs and so require a strong hand to get them to do what YOU want rather than what THEY want. Whether buying or adopting a Beagle, it's important to be ready to have a plan for training.

If you're adopting a Beagle, be aware of all health and behavioral problems that Beagle may have, but understand that any Beagle may be unlucky enough to have a health problem or an owner that overfeeds him or an owner that doesn't train him. When you adopt a Beagle, you are giving that pup a chance at happiness with a loving and responsible owner.

CHAPTER 3
Preparing Your Home for Your Beagle

"It is so important to be prepared and ready before you bring your new puppy home. From having the correct food, setting up a vet visit, and ensuring your home is ready for your new puppy.   Being prepared and ready will make the transition for you and your new puppy so much easier and enjoyable."

Linda Tordai
TheBeagleBarn.com

Photo Courtesy of Beth Forbey

After you've chosen your new pup and before you actually bring him home, it's important that your home, the Beagle's soon-to-be new home, has been prepared for his arrival.

The first thing that needs to be done is preparing the current residents of your home for the new family member. That includes any other adults, children, and current pets. While you are giving a Beagle a new home, you should ensure those already living in your home have as comfortable and safe a transition as your new housemate does.

That isn't to say that you should automatically start worrying about incidents happening. If you're looking to add a new pet to your family, you likely already know how well your current pets and your children get along with new animals.

Introducing a New Beagle to Current Pets

When introducing your new Beagle to your other pets, it's important to remember that every animal is different, and even if your cats or dogs have liked other dogs in the past, that doesn't mean they will like this new dog. If your current pets have had traumatic experiences with dogs in the past, either consult a pet therapist before proceeding, reconsider getting a dog or proceed with caution.

Take into consideration the personalities of both your current pets and your new pet to plan for introductions. If you know you have an excitable and friendly dog at home, but your new Beagle seems scared or reserved, you'll want to introduce the two slowly so you can teach your pets how to respectfully interact with each other.

Thankfully for me, my two cats adjusted to Arthur relatively quickly. My older cat has lived with other dogs before, but my younger cat was

Photo Courtesy of
Judy Varin

Photo Courtesy of Hannah Flagg

rescued from the street and has had some negative interactions with dogs in the past. Despite his history with dogs, the younger cat tolerates Arthur's presence in the house, and I've even caught them playing on occasion. Beagles are friendly enough to sneak through anyone's defenses, especially during playtime.

You might find even the most reserved of your animals becoming friends with your new Beagle after a few months.

Introducing a New Beagle to Children

If this Beagle is your first pet and your children don't have experience around animals, you should keep a few things in mind to keep both your children and your new pup safe.

Let your children know, before the new dog arrives, that they are to be calm and patient in their interactions with the new family member. New puppies between the ages of eight and 10 weeks are easily fearful, and your Beagle has yet to explore his new home or or meet the whole family. Give him time to adjust to his new surroundings without overwhelming him.

Let your new friend come walk to meet everyone on his own terms. Tell your children not to run up to the new Beagle puppy or startle him and to, overall, let him initiate interactions at first. Dogs have their own "personal bubbles," and if you're in a part of a dog's bubble that they consider to be intimate, they may react negatively just like a human might if you stood too closely to them. There are new sights, new sounds, and new smells, and I guarantee that as soon as your Beagle pup gets comfortable, he will be off exploring every scent he can find, including yours.

A great way to teach your children the proper way to interact with the new puppy is to let them see you interacting with the puppy properly. Children will imitate the behaviors they see you display. If little Suze sees you slipping your new Beagle puppy a slice of bacon in the morning, you could easily have her sneaking the unwanted portions of her own meals to the puppy as a treat, so beware.

As you and your children walk, feed, train, and clean up after your puppy together, you will establish good habits as you teach both your children and your new puppy good habits.

Until you know how well your children handle the new Beagle and how well the new Beagle interact with your children, you should be sure to stay close by to watch over both parties, but don't interrupt unless the situation seems to be taking a bad turn.

Dangerous Things That Dogs Might Eat

"Because they are driven by food, and they explore the world with their nose and their mouth, they will -- and do -- eat anything."

Dennis Dollar
Barrister Beagles

Sweet and Store-Bought Snacks

These foods are a treat for you, but they aren't usually healthy for you, and they sure as heck aren't good for your dog. Some sweets can even be fatal to your dear family member, so consider cutting a few of these tasty, but dangerous treats from your family's diet.

Snacks	Symptoms
Chocolate (especially dark chocolate and cooking chocolate)	Seizures, vomiting, diarrhea, uncontrolled urination (potentially fatal)
Macadamia nuts (which may be in cookies)	Lethargy, vomiting, fever, tremors
Any food item containing the sweetener Xylitol (diet foods, store-bought baked goods, candy, gum, etc.)	"Drunk-like" behavior, liver failure, vomiting, increased heart rate, seizures
Anything containing nutmeg (pies, cakes, cookies)	Increased heart rate, dry mouth, seizures, stomach pain, disorientation

Fruits and Vegetables

Most fresh fruits and veggies are perfectly fine for our furry companions and can even be a vital part of their diets. Both you and your pets should partake in fruits and veggies, but make sure to keep the following out of your pup's diet.

Fruits and Vegetables	Symptoms
Onions, garlic, other alliums	Anemia, (potentially fatal)
Grapes/raisins	Kidney failure, lethargy, dehydration, vomiting, diarrhea
Any part of an avocado plant including the fruit, bark, stems, and leaves	Vomiting and diarrhea; (fatal in large quantities)
Lemons/limes	Vomiting, diarrhea

Animal Products

Unsurprisingly, most animal products are perfectly fine to feed your dog, but be sure to only feed your pup the freshest and best-quality meats.

Animal Products	Symptoms
Mishandled raw meat	Diarrhea, vomiting, abdominal pain
Chicken bones	Bleeding, vomiting, drooling, moving oddly

Drinks

With the exception of a few drinks made specifically for dogs, avoid giving your pup anything other than water, and be sure he doesn't drink any of the following that you have sitting around.

Drinks	Symptoms
Coffee/tea	Seizures, vomiting, diarrhea, uncontrolled urination, (potentially fatal)
Any caffeinated soft drink	Seizures, vomiting, diarrhea,
Alcohol	Lethargy, vomiting, shortness of breath/panting
Saltwater	Vomiting, diarrhea, tremors, seizures

Other Household Dangers

Dogs can get into more than just our trash cans and dinner plates. There are potential dangers all over the home for the unwary dog owner. Keeping your new Beagle safe means keeping the following things out of reach of your pets.

Potential Hazards to Avoid
Human/pet medicines
Insecticides/pesticides
Some plants/fertilizers
Antifreeze/deicers/oil
Paint/paint thinner
Batteries/cords
Household cleaners/oven cleaner/detergents

Photo Courtesy of Emily Jarvis

Preparing a Space for Your Dog Inside

Your Beagle pup will likely be anxious when she first arrives at her new home regardless of whether she's coming from a shelter, a store, or a breeder's home.

Beagles are naturally playful and friendly, so even if the pup was excited to be leaving her old home with you, she may still be nervous in a new place that's much bigger than the small space she shared with her littermates.

To make your dog feel more secure, be sure that you've prepared a space specifically for her inside your home. Remember that dogs prefer small, quiet, and enclosed spaces. This space should be away from the other pets at first and should already have some of the dog's new things waiting for her.

Clean and clear this space of any potentially dangerous chemicals or anything your new Beagle may get her teeth on. Beagles love to chew, and they will chew on whatever they find.

A laundry room is a good option and may be easier to clean compared to other areas of your home, but any room or enclosed area will suffice. Beware, though! Beagles are surprisingly high jumpers once they gain the confidence to make the attempt. My early attempts at DIY pet gates were quickly mastered.

When we brought Arthur home, waiting for him was a crate with a plush dog bed inside. We'd let him choose a few toys from the pet store before we brought him home, and by the end of the night, I'd given him my favorite soft blanket to keep him comfortable in his new home.

Beagles are small dogs, and it's smart to keep kennels proportional to the size of the dog, especially puppies in the process of being house-trained. Dogs also don't like to spoil an area they consider to be theirs, so giving your new Beagle her own space is more than just for making her comfortable; it's one of the first steps to properly house-training your new Beagle.

Here are a few supplies I suggest you have on hand:

- A crate
- Chew toys
- Treats
- A pet bed
- Puppy pads
- Pet-safe cleaning spray
- Paper towels

Preparing Outside Spaces

Outside areas are equally as important as inside areas, especially if you find yourself with a Beagle who likes to sneak off to do her business in the house to avoid cold, wet, or otherwise-unpleasant weather like mine did.

To ensure the comfort and safety of your new family member while she's outside, prepare an enclosed area for play and potty. If you don't have a fenced-in area for your Beagle to roam, don't leave her alone or unleashed. Again, it doesn't take much to entice a Beagle to track a scent.

Even if your yard is fenced in, you'll want to indicate a specific area of the yard for your pup to do her business, especially if you and your family use your backyard often.

To let your Beagle know what areas of the yard are for her specific purposes, utilize pet pens and gates which are sold in various sizes, or just guide her to the area you want her to do her business. Her play area should have a water bowl and plenty of shade from the sun.

If you have activity areas in your yard, check to see if there's anything your dog could get into. Examples include grills/charcoal, insecticides/weed killer, uncovered pools/pool cleaner, compost piles/gardens.

A few weeks into getting Arthur, I was turning my compost and Arthur hurriedly ate a few clumps of the dirt that had fallen out. I shooed him away and cleaned the mess, but a few hours later, Arthur was sick and we were at the vet. I realized he had gotten a clump of dirt that happened to have ground coffee, and even though Arthur was fine, with no long-term problems, I was conscious of making our yard as safe for him as possible.

HELPFUL TIP
Keep an Eye on Him!

The Beagle can be mischievous and get himself into trouble. Keep an eye on your dog so that he doesn't have the chance to wander off. Set boundaries for your new pet, but also be proactive by putting up the garbage can, keeping "people" food out of his reach, and not crowding him while he is eating. Try not to play tug-of-war with your Beagle. This type of interaction may cause the dog to get overexcited, snapping and scratching you inadvertently. Beagles are also known "diggers," so place houseplants out of reach.

If the backyard is just the territory of your pets, make sure they don't have access to animal feces or corpses. Consider scheduling daily or weekly cleanups of your yard, or invest in another cleaning treatment. Animals live and die around buildings such as garages and sheds, and Beagles were bred to discover and eat small game, even if the rodents they're hunting now are different from the hares their ancestors retrieved.

Fleas, ticks, and other pests are also a concern. If your yard is somewhat untamed or you live in a flea-heavy area, invest in pet-safe yard treatments and keep the grass and foliage trimmed and clear of leaves or other debris.

If you live in an area in which the wilderness overflows into your yard or neighborhood, be cautious of wild animals who may wander into your yard, regardless of if you have a fence.

CHAPTER 4
Bringing Home Your Beagle

"Bring home your beagle is much like bringing home a new baby. They expect constant attention and structure. Patience is the most important. I always tell people your first few weeks are the hardest."

Linda Tordai
TheBeagleBarn.com

The Ride Home

Photo Courtesy of Deborah Smith

The ride home is a special event for both you and your new puppy. He has no idea where he's going, but he's excited and nervous to go on an adventure. He's experiencing new sights and new smells, and you're involved and delighting in all of his discoveries.

Your first car ride home with your Beagle puppy shouldn't be complicated. To ensure the ride is a safe and memorable one, check how long your drive will be so you can plan potty stops.

Consider a travel crate for the first and future rides. When bringing home your new Beagle, you should have a safe way to transport him in the car. A travel crate may be the most stable option, but you could also a pet cage, pet carrier, or

Photo Courtesy of
Toby Thompson and Lianne Mott

just a simple seatbelt harness. Be sure to select the correctly-sized option for your Beagle.

Once you and your puppy are ready to set off toward home, remember not to put your new young family member in the front seat. Not only could a blow from the airbags injure or kill your beloved pet, but it may also be harder to keep your puppy calm and undistracted in the front seat with all the windows showing him something new. In turn, your exploring pup may distract the driver. Instead, recruit someone to use treats and toys to keep your Beagle interested and occupied in the backseat.

Beagles are known for carsickness, especially if they're traveling after a meal. If you're bringing your new puppy home, he likely hasn't eaten much or anything, so the first ride may not be one that results in vomiting, but know that the signs of carsickness in dogs include excessive drooling, whining, yawning, and vomiting. Combine a stable travel carrier with a car toy or two to make the ride easier.

The Importance of Having a Plan

Photo Courtesy of Christi Berry

Having a plan not only for transporting your new Beagle home but also for the first night home is important. You don't want to be caught off guard when something unexpected happens with your new puppy. There will definitely be messes and tumbles and whimpers, but as long as you have a plan for anything that truly goes wrong, your first night should be a success.

A dog is a commitment for everyone in the household. By this point, everyone should know a new house member is soon arriving, but also make sure everyone knows what to expect with first introductions and for the first few days.

Predetermine areas the new Beagle is and isn't allowed to go. If pets aren't allowed on the furniture, prepare everyone in the household to help train the new puppy on house rules. With Beagles, it's especially important to have a treat schedule outside of training times and to restrict human food and overeating. Every member of the household should know these rules before bringing your new pet home.

Decide on the following ahead of time, and brainstorm some unique considerations your own family may have:

- where the new puppy will sleep
- where his food and water are kept
- where you will keep his crate
- where he will go potty
- who will do which pet chores
- who is primarily in charge of training
- how often training will occur
- where training will happen
- who will be the primary veterinarian

The first night is also the best time to get your new Beagle on a routine, and you should have any planned routines ready to be set into motion when your Beagle walks through the door of its forever home.

Photo Courtesy of Abby Myers

While planning, be sure to have some pet supplies ready and waiting at home. You won't want to bother with leaving the house a lot and risk destructive behavior because you forgot something at the store.

Pet supplies to have ready are things such as a leash, harness, collar and ID tag, chew toys, doggie bags for walks, puppy pads for house training, and pet odor/stain-removing cleaning spray.

The First Night Home

A puppy's first night in a new home can be exciting and scary. He's learning his name, meeting new people, and seeing new places. With a plan, the first night home can be a joyously quiet occasion with as few stresses as possible.

You should expect anxiety from your new Beagle this first night. After all, even though your home is his new home as well, he hasn't yet been far from either his mother and littermate or his kennel mates. Dogs are pack animals, and your Beagle is far from the only pack he's ever known. It will take time to for him to get used to the new pack and home.

To cut down on anxiety and prevent howling, whining, and scratching, make your puppy feel secure. The areas you've set up for your dog, inside and out, will serve to help him feel more secure, especially if this area is in a more public area since dogs, especially Beagle puppies, do not like to be isolated from the rest of their pack—which now includes you and your family.

As soon as you've settled your pup down, show him where his food, water, and potty areas are. Your puppy will probably need to relieve him-

Photo Courtesy of
Magda Nawrot

self if he hasn't already done so in the house or on the ride home. A short walk to the designated outside potty area before bedtime will help establish a house-training and sleep routine.

At least for the first few nights, let your puppy sleep in his crate if you intend to crate train. Your puppy is likely to whine and cry a lot if he is left to sleep alone in a crate or in his designated area, but in order to get your pup used to separation and sleeping alone, you should ignore these cries until your pup falls asleep. Chew toys, plush toys, and pillows can help ease anxiety. Many pet stores sell "heartbeat" pillows that simulate the beat of a mother's heart. Your puppy will eventually get used to sleeping alone.

Throughout the night, your puppy will likely wake up needing to go to the bathroom, so be alert to his stirring in the night, or you're sure to wake up to a mess.

First Vet Visit/Choosing a Vet

Within the first week, you'll want to take your new Beagle to a vet. Some breeders require that you do so in your contracts with them, but in general, it's a good idea to gauge your pet's health if you weren't presented with medical history when you bought or adopted your pet. It's also a good idea to see a vet ASAP so you can start a good relationship with a vet you trust with your precious family member before an emergency actually arises.

If you've already got a veterinarian from previous pets, taking your new Beagle to that vet is a good idea as you will already have a relationship.

If you don't yet have an established vet, choosing one can be confusing or overwhelming. To find a new vet, reach out to family, friends, coworkers, neighbors, and anyone else you know who is a pet parent. Established pet parents have been there, done that when it comes to finding a good vet, and most of them will know which vets they love and which you should absolutely not visit.

See what veterinarians your local animal shelters or rescue groups recommend. Shelters deal with injured animals often, and not all of them have in-house veterinarians. The American Animal Hospital Association is another resource to utilize when searching for a new veterinarian; you can search the association's website for accredited veterinarian offices near you.

If you find yourself with many options for a vet, think about what's important to you. You may not find the right vet the first time, but keep looking for the right office. If you plan early enough, you can even visit several vets before you've officially brought home your pet.

The first thing to consider is the location of the vet. Somewhere closer to home may be convenient.

HELPFUL TIP
Have a Plan:
Choosing a Vet

Before you bring your Beagle home, do some research on choosing a veterinarian. By asking friends and family members, you may be steered in the right direction. You'll want to have a vet who has a location near you and hours that are compatible with your schedule. Don't be afraid to check online reviews for vets and veterinary hospitals in your area. Ask yourself what you are able to afford and check prices at various animal hospitals. Are busier veterinary hospitals usually worth the wait? Some say yes, but do your homework. The American Animal Hospital Association (AAHA), established in 1933, accredits veterinary hospitals. Nearly 3,000 veterinary hospitals are accredited by the AAHA in the United States and Canada.

Once you're actually inside of your vet's office, keep your eyes open. Are the rooms clean? Is there soap at the sinks? Does the office seem organized?

Consider the friendliness of the staff—these are the people who will be helping take care of your pet and who will be interacting with you on every visit. Look out for a calm demeanor and professionalism. Do they seem to know what they're talking about? Include the veterinarian when you're making these considerations, of course.

While at the vet, figure out what services the vet offers and which services you'll have to go somewhere else for. These services include emergency services as most vet offices do not have overnight care, even in an emergency situation. Keep in mind the cost of services at that vet, as well as any credit-line opportunities in case of emergencies.

*Photo Courtesy of
Reagan Ann Brodersen*

Puppy Classes

Puppy classes are an excellent idea for both you and your pet. Not only are these classes a good opportunity for you and your pet to learn the commands that create a well-trained dog, but they are also an opportunity for your and your pup to socialize with other dogs and dog parents.

During these classes, held one to two times a week, depending on the class, the trainer teaches owners how to command their pets, and then sends them home to practice. This time walking around, trying to convince your Beagle to sit, is a good way to meet new people in your situation as well as to trade training tips and pet stories. Additionally, your Beagle will receive the vital socialization young dogs need to be well-rounded and adjusted.

Cost Breakdown for the First Year

Depending on the current health of your pet, the area in which you live, the vet you choose to take your pet to, and the products you choose to use, your costs for the first year can run between $365 and $1,193.

Expense	Estimated Cost
Vaccinations	$100-$268
Physical Exam	$45-$60
Dental Cleaning	$75-$125
Spay/Neuter	$35-$400
Heartworm Testing/Prevention	$45-$130
Flea Treatment	$40-$150
Fecal Exam	$25-$60
Total	**$365-$1,193**

This cost may seem high, but it's a small one to pay for the health and medical safety of a member of your family. There are many low-cost pet clinics and options for discounted spaying and neutering. Most shelters will list such resources on their websites.

CHAPTER 5
Being a Puppy Parent

Standing by Your Expectations

Everyone has their own expectations about what having a new puppy will be like. Some things I expected before bringing Arthur home were lots of evening walks with plenty of playtime and cuddles during the day.

My expectation of playtime and cuddle time were exceeded; Arthur loves all of his toys, and he loves jumping onto the couch to warm up with his pack, but walks? He likes them occasionally, especially if there are new smells in our neighborhood, but he would much rather stay home and lounge in the backyard. I don't mind the lack of walks too much, though I was hoping for an excuse to exercise more.

I wasn't too disappointed that one of my expectations wasn't met, but I didn't have too many of them, and none of them were related to the realities of new parenthood. I've had pets for over 10 years, so I know that a new pet comes with new stresses as well as new joys.

Many people have expectations of what life with their new puppy will be like, and sometimes the reality is unpleasant. The reality of puppy parenthood has resulted in the return of some pets, so it's important for you to be ready right off the bat for some, if not all, of your expectations to fall through.

One expectation that many people have is that they'll cuddle with their new pup, especially since Beagles are pack animals. While Beagles do enjoy napping and relaxing together, more often than not they want to run around, while you want to cuddle. These pups are so full of energy, with little time to rest when there are boxes to chew on and couches to jump off the back of.

People also think that training won't take much time, but with Beagles, you should be prepared for a stubborn dog who won't do anything unless you're offering food. It may be frustrating to have this experience of a disobedient dog when you just want to enjoy your new friend, and it is discouraging, but a Beagle can be trained eventually.

The fastest way to eliminate most of the new stressors that come with being a new puppy parent is to face the realities of puppy parenthood. It takes work and training to adapt to the realities of new puppies, but training can make your expectation of a polite and companionable pet a reality.

Work to meet these new expectations, and they will become reality.

Photo Courtesy of Brittany Helton

45

Why Crate Train

The Beagle has had centuries of behavior development. Although you can't "out train" unwanted behaviors in this pack dog, you can avoid aggressive conduct with knowledge and patience. Avoid aggressive play like chasing, wrestling, and playing tug-of-war. Beagles aren't happy to sit around the house all day and may exhibit signs of boredom like chewing or digging. Your companion wants to play and needs to be taken on frequent walks. Is he destructive when home alone? He may be suffering from separation anxiety. Although an independent breed, Beagles crave their owners' companionship. Watch for signs and ask a professional for help if needed.

Proper crate training can be highly effective in the training of your Beagle and is useful not only for preventing destructive behavior but also for helping your pup become house-trained. You won't have a well-trained dog on the first night and, in fact, it can take months of mindful training before your Beagle is trained. Crate training allows you to control your pup's environment during these important early stages in your Beagle's behavioral training and will shorten the overall training time.

Although crate training greatly helps with a dog's behavioral training, training, in general, should not be the primary use of the crate. A dog's crate is like a human's room—it's a place for him to go to relax and get away from the other members of the house or from outside stimuli and can give your dog a sense of security. These benefits of crating don't appear immediately, though. First, you must introduce your new Beagle to her crate and teach her what it's for and when she should enter it. Everything in your home is new to your dog, including her new crate, so it's important to make your dog's first impressions of the crate good ones.

The most important part of crate training is the crate itself. The crate you buy for a dog should be proportional to her current size, with room for growth. She should have room to stand up and walk in a circle, but if she has more room, she'll use a corner as a potty area. If the "room-for-growth" crate you purchase doesn't come with a space divider, make plans for a DIY one at home.

For a Beagle, a 36-inch crate should be sufficient. I, personally, suggest a crate with multiple doors if your local pet store has that option. I found myself moving Arthur's crate around too much before I began utilizing both doors and placed the crate in an optimal position to access both.

If you have a more compact living space, being able to open a door from a long side or a short side means you can squeeze this equally-compact crate almost anywhere. I've put mine under tables and used it as an area divider to make a puppy playpen.

Overall, you want to find a good spot to place your dog's crate such as in a corner of the family/living area of the house. Again, dogs are pack animals and want to feel as if they are part of your pack.

Crate Training

Now that you've chosen a good crate for your Beagle, it's time to introduce her to her new room. Make sure the crate door is open and inviting before this introduction!

The first time your pup sees her new crate, she may be cautious to approach and enter it. Caution is fine. Your pup will eventually explore the crate herself, without you interfering, especially if you've put toys, a bed, and/or blankets inside. If your pup still seems cautious about entering, carry her over, speaking soothingly and happily to put her at ease.

With any dog, but especially Beagles, putting a few strategically-placed treats inside is another way to make a crate more inviting. Start with a few treats just outside the crate, place some just inside the door, and then give your pup a treat and praise her if she completely enters the crate. Try the same technique with her food bowl if snacks just aren't cutting it.

It's important that you're patient and don't force your Beagle into the crate. You don't want your new friend to feel trapped in a place that's supposed to be safe for her. If she doesn't enter the crate all the way or at all on the first try, just give her time. It may even take your pup a few days to feel fully comfortable going inside her crate.

After your Beagle pup has gotten used to her crate, you'll want to start feeding her in her crate as well. Doing so is another step in making your Beagle's crate feel like HER crate. Eventually, you'll be able to close the crate door for short periods of time either while your pup is inside relaxing or inside eating.

Sit next to your Beagle's crate for short periods of time while she's inside. Consider reading or some other activity that you normally do. You want your Beagle to understand that being inside her crate is nothing to be worried about and is just a normal part of your lives. As your Beagle gets used to her crate, begin taking small trips away from the crate during your crate-sitting time. Go make a cup of tea, use the restroom, or just stretch your legs. Your pup will eventually become used to your ab-

Photo Courtesy of
Larissa Pyer

sence, and you'll be able to leave her alone for longer and longer stretches of time.

You need to be consistent about when you're crating. When I'm cooking dinner, gardening, working, sleeping, or otherwise busy are typically the times when I utilize the crate.

Remember that a crate is not a long-term daycare for your pup, so crate time should be limited to no more than 30 minutes at a time. You can increase this time as your puppy grows in age and becomes more comfortable being left alone in general. Eventually, she'll be peacefully sleeping in her crate through the night and will quietly and happily rest in her crate if you ever need to run errands.

Your pup will likely whine at many points before crate training is complete; that's just a reality. These whines will be adorably sad and will make you want to give your Beagle whatever she wants. Beagles have such a beautifully pleading expression, and an added whine makes them hard to deny.

Regardless, you must not give in to your dog's whining! If your pup whines during her training, it may be because she's feeling uncomfortable in the crate at that time and is ready to be let out. Early in the crate-training process, whines let you know your pup's limits. Don't let your Beagle out of her crate immediately when she whines. You don't want to teach her that whining will get her what she wants. Wait until she's settled down again, then let her out of her crate.

I find that as long as Arthur is in his crate in the public area, he's not bothered about being inside while everyone is busy. He may whine a bit, but he's learned by now that he's safe in his crate.

Remember that a crate should be a safe place for your Beagle. Your puppy should not be afraid to go into her crate. Whining to be let out, once inside for timeout, is a different matter. Beagles aren't afraid to let everyone within hearing distance know their displeasure, but gentle whining is rarely something to be worried about, even if it will trigger your parenting senses.

Keep this information in mind as you repeat this process for the first few weeks of your Beagle's new life, and your Beagle will love to go inside her crate and will be less likely to whine and howl when you have to leave her alone.

Chewing

There's a reason that parents and pet owners alike are both known for shouting, "What are you eating?!" at least 20 times a day. Kids and pups alike both love exploring the world, and many do so by chomping on anything they can find, and for the first six months of your Beagle's life, his gums will periodically bother him as he experiences teething. As such, your Beagle is guaranteed to chew on whatever he can find if he's a puppy, so make sure you've prepped plenty of toys that he can chew on. Adult dogs, however, may chew for other reasons such as improper training, boredom, attention-seeking, and fear or anxiety.

Besides the above reasons for chewing, some Beagles just seem to have an overwhelming drive to explore the world by chewing.

One of the Beagle's primary instincts is to sniff out treasures, usually rabbits. Some Beagles naturally will just steal whatever they find and not chew on it. Instead, they'll run off to abandon their find somewhere or run to gift it to another member of the pack. "Retrieving" isn't too usual for Beagles, though, so you should be prepared to find your stolen item chewed up somewhere if you don't recover it quickly.

My household had prepared well for Arthur's arrival in terms of cords and other dangerous things a Beagle might find his way into, but even still, for the first three months of having Arthur, I found some of the following items around the house that had been retrieved and/or left chewed up:

- Cardboard boxes
- Napkins and paper towels
- Socks
- My mom's sweater that I was mending
- My half of a pizza heart necklace
- An emery board
- Yarn
- Pillows

Though retrieving can look quite adorable (because who doesn't like to see a floppy-eared pup running down the hall with a sock in his mouth?), it's important that you discourage this behavior, even when your Beagle has taken a harmless item like a hanging kitchen towel or a fallen paper towel.

These items may seem harmless, but the behavior itself also has the potential to cause trouble. Your Beagle may become used to retrieving whatever he pleases; then he will be at risk of chewing on or eating something dangerous.

Additionally, if you regularly allow your dog to retrieve and do as he pleases with everything he retrieves and then attempt to take something from him, your dog may become aggressive. In his mind, everything he retrieves is his because you haven't stopped him before and taught him otherwise. This behavior can be extremely dangerous for you and your Beagle. Your Beagle may retrieve and chew on something dangerous that you are unable to take from him because of his aggression, and you may both be hurt in the process.

I mentioned earlier that a necklace of mine fell victim to Arthur's retrieving. Unfortunately, I didn't realize I'd dropped the necklace as I was in the middle of cleaning, and I was letting Arthur roam around to "help" me. While most of the necklace was fine, the pizza charm looked like pizza party leftovers. Keep your things safe if you don't want them chewed!

Dogs also like to chew on their companions, but you should discourage your Beagle from chewing or biting people. A puppy's bite may not hurt at first, but it will definitely get stronger with age. Teach your pup to be gentle with humans. If your pup chews your hand, you should discourage this behavior over time by "yelping" whenever your pup takes a nibble at your hands.

Photo Courtesy of Casey Murdough

Of course, you should also teach your Beagle what is and is not acceptable to chew. Again, you should have toys for your pup that he is allowed to chew on. When you take a harmless item from your pup, reprimand him and offer him something that is acceptable to chew on such as a teething ring or plush toy.

Do NOT give your dog DIY toys that are similar to what you don't want him stealing. Examples of a bad DIY toy are an old shoe, socks, rags, old clothes, etc. Your Beagle will not be able to distinguish these "acceptable-to-chew" items from the "unacceptable-to-chew" items.

Ultimately, it is your responsibility to make sure anything that shouldn't be in your dog's mouth stays out of it, including your hands and feet! Be sure to discourage your pup from chewing on people early on, to avoid dangerous and tragic incidents later on.

Be sure that you've provided a variety of textures for your pup to explore early on. If you see that he's stealing a lot of hard things like wooden spoons or pencils, find him a toy with that same consistency. Also, make chewing part of playtime with tug toys or snack time with chewy snacks. Playtime will help tire your Beagle out, and both activities will help satisfy your Beagle's need to chomp.

Growling, Barking, and Howling

Dogs naturally growl and bark in various situations, including during playtime, but, of course, growling and barking can also be aggressive. Let's first distinguish between playful behavior, aggressive behavior, and other potential causes of growling, barking, and howling. Addressing this behavior can take time and consistency as with all of your Beagle's training.

It's important to know that Beagles are naturally vocal dogs, so growling, barking, and howling may not always be a sign of aggression. Regardless, Beagles are also very LOUD dogs, so you want to discourage occurrences of inappropriate growling, barking, and howling, or you're sure to get complaints from neighbors. After some time living with your Beagle, you will be able to distinguish the meaning of many of his sounds from his standard bark to his aggressive bark and his "alert howl" to his "I'm sad and/or bored" howl.

Growling

Growling is just one of the ways dogs communicate and is actually an important communication for you to maintain in your dog since she can't use words to tell you when something is wrong.

There are times when your dog is growling because she is being playful (such as when you're playing tug), but growling is sometimes an indication of another problem that needs to be understood and addressed before the growling will stop. Growling itself should NOT be stopped, though, because it's your dog's way of warning you that something is wrong and that she may bite. If you eliminate growling from your dog's behavior, you won't know when something is wrong, and your dog may attack unexpectedly. Be careful around your dog until you figure out why she's growling.

Your pup may growl if she's in pain. Painful growling is usually accompanied by other symptoms of illness or injury. If pain is the cause of growling, get your pup proper treatment. Your veterinarian can help you figure out the source of your dog's pain.

Dogs often growl as a warning when they feel as if someone is encroaching on their territory. This "someone" could be a stranger who steps onto your property, or it may be another pet that lay down in your pup's favorite spot. Similarly, your dog may growl if someone is too close to or has one of her possessions. Such possessions include toys, food bowls, treats, and anything the dog considers to be her own.

Fear of strangers or specific people can make your dog growl. Fireworks, thunderstorms, garbage day, or vacuuming may be sometimes when your pup growls.

To treat warning growling and fearful growling, acclimate your Beagle to whatever is triggering the growling. Your dog may need more socialization if she often growls at strange people or dogs. If your dog is barking at something she's afraid of, either remove that fear trigger or allow your dog to see that something like the vacuum cleaner isn't scary.

Simply put, growling itself can't and shouldn't be treated, so to stop specific types of growling, analyze why your dog is growling in the first place.

Barking

Barking is another way dogs communicate, so it can mean something different depending on the context. Often, dogs will bark to greet a human or another animal or in order to get another animal to play. Barking in and of itself is not a problem. One way to control the problem is to just ignore it as dogs often bark to gain attention, but excessive barking definitely can be caused by a bigger problem than attention-seeking, so be proactive about controlling excessive barking, especially if you have neighbors.

Just like with growling, dogs will bark if they are feeling territorial or protective over something such as an area or item they consider theirs.

A startled or afraid dog will also bark. Fearful barks can range from short, surprised back to constant barking at whatever may be scaring your pup. Fearful barking can happen anywhere your dog feels unsafe or afraid. Fearful barking can stem from separation anxiety as well. A dog with separation anxiety will bark excessively while left alone.

A simple way to stop barking is to firmly interrupt your dog's barking with a single word and to reward your pup once he stops barking. I use the word "hey!" and some people say "quiet!" but the word itself doesn't matter, as long as your Beagle is able to recognize, by the command and the tone of your voice, that you mean business. Consistency with interrupting barking will prevent it overall.

Boredom and loneliness are also reasons a dog may bark. Play with and tire out your dog before you leave the house if you know your dog barks excessively while you're away. If your dog barks while you're away because of separation anxiety, you will likely need to consult your veterinarian. Separation anxiety is usually accompanied by other behaviors including digging and destructiveness.

Howling

Howling isn't a problem every dog owner will have, but a Beagle owner should definitely be prepared for howling. Just like with growling and barking, howling is a way dogs communicate what they're feeling.

Howling is caused by a Beagle's strong hunting instincts. Beagles used to be expected and encouraged to howl to help hunters find them once the Beagles had found their prey, but this instinct isn't so great when you're not on the hunt or have no plans to ever do so as in the case of a family dog.

Beagles are used to howling during a hunt, but you may notice that your Beagle is howling a lot even if you and your family aren't attending many hunts. Many other things can make your Beagle howl including excitement, stress, loneliness, boredom, attention-seeking, or just plain fun.

If you're not taking your buddy on hunts with you, you'll want to curb this instinct to howl unless you and your neighbors really enjoy the piercing noise of an excited Beagle.

Just like with growling and barking, the way to stop howling is to determine the reason your Beagle is howling in the first place and address that problem.

Do your neighbors report that your Beagle is howling excessively while you're gone? If so, your pup is likely lonely and in want of affection and attention. Beagles do not do well alone, and while radios and TVs in the background may be an option to make your pup feel less lonely, remember that Beagles love being with their packs—meaning your Beagle will love being with you and your family and will be sad if he isn't with you.

Other pets, specifically dogs, can prevent howling caused by loneliness. If you have another dog at home to keep your Beagle company, he won't spend so much time howling for his pack to return to him.

Boredom is another problem that can make your Beagle howl and can affect your Beagle whether you're home or not.

Beagles are used to being put to work, and even though many Beagles will also enjoy a family lifestyle, they still need to put their natural energy to use somehow.

Howling is one way that your Beagle will entertain himself and use up energy at the same time, so spend some time burning off excess energy with your pup by going on runs, playing catch, and other creative playtime activities. Your pup can't howl if he's got a toy in his mouth, and he won't want to howl when he's exhausted from playtime.

A great strategy that I use successfully to discourage excessive growling, barking, or howling is to simply interrupt the behavior with a loud sound, a light spray of water, or with an interruption word like "hey!" or "quiet!" Usually, all that's needed is to get your pup's attention while using an unmistakably "bad dog" voice.

Overall, you should expect a lot of sounds from your Beagle. While this breed is small, they are incredibly expressive beyond just their surprisingly loud growl, bark, and howl.

Digging

Like many other dog breeds, Beagles love to dig. Beagles will dig inside or outside, and both can cause problems for a Beagle owner. Dogs dig, by instinct, to create a nest or to hide food (or chew toys and treats).

A big reason dogs dig is because they are bored. Inside or out, if your Beagle has nothing to do, he will create an activity for himself. Digging is an activity that entertains your dog and works off energy, but it can leave your yard and Beagle both a muddy mess.

The most obvious answer to this problem is to provide outdoor entertainment for your dog; toys are fun to play with, but many dog toys also require a human to throw or pull for them to be fun.

Treats that take a long time to eat or get to are another option to keep your dog distracted from digging, but many Beagles also just dig for fun. You may have to train your dog to only dig in certain areas of the yard if he can't give up digging altogether. If you do designate a digging area, hide some toys and treats under loosely-covered soil in the area you set aside and encourage him to dig in that area alone.

The "Playtime" chapter of this book gives more ideas about how to entertain your Beagle both inside and out.

A dog may also dig because he knows digging may get him freedom from, say, a gated yard.

Beagles are escape artists, and digging is a tool a Beagle will use to his advantage to aid in his escapes. If you've got any low or weak areas around your fence, be prepared for digging once your pup discovers those weaknesses.

Don't feel sad if your Beagle tries to escape often—he's likely just trying to follow a scent that he's caught. Beagles can't really help but investigate an interesting scent.

To discourage digging at the fence, it's advisable to block off the fence perimeter. Some owners have used cement blocks to line their fences; some have worked chicken wire into the bottom of the fencing. Either option works to prevent digging in this area.

If a dog is digging in a specific area and seems to be searching for something, you may have rodents in your yard that you need to deal with. If the sun shines harshly into your yard and there's not much shade, your dog may dig to find shelter from the sun.

Overall, some ways to prevent digging include walking your dog daily, playing active games with your dog, keeping fun and interactive toys available to your dog, providing shade for your dog to rest in outside, and keeping an eye on your dog while outside, to watch for digging.

Additionally, your dog just may feel anxious in the backyard if he's alone there often and may dig under the gate the same way a fearful dog may destructively dig at inside carpets and doors. If you find that anxiety is the cause of digging, you need to treat your dog's separation anxiety to prevent digging.

Separation Anxiety

The Beagle is a pack dog that really does enjoy being with its family. Left alone, without the feeling of safety that comes from being with her pack, your Beagle may lose control of her emotions, believing that you are never returning and that she will be alone forever.

Beagles are likely to experience separation anxiety, so it's important to start early with getting your Beagle used to your absence. Separation anxiety is accompanied by whining, excessive barking, destructive chewing, excessive digging, howling, and other panicky actions.

Oftentimes, dog owners discover their dog's separation anxiety only after returning home to a huge mess, destroyed property, and a crying pup, which can be heartbreaking, stressful, and frustrating all at once.

Treating separation anxiety takes time and patience.

If your dog does have separation anxiety, you may see signs of it even when you are home. Are you able to go to the bathroom without your Beagle whining at the door? Do you find yourself tripping over your pup every time you enter a room because she can't bear to be away from you? Your pup may be anxious that she won't see you again if she lets you out of her sight.

Addressing Separation Anxiety

Separation anxiety typically sets in within 20 minutes of your dog being alone, so having something to occupy your pup for that period of time can help lessen her anxiety while you're away.

The first step to addressing separation anxiety is to consider the area in which your dog will be spending time away from you alone.

Many people assume that giving their dog the run of the house while they are away will give their dog less reason to be bored, but really all they are doing is maximizing the number of things their dog has access to destroy.

Often, having the entire house to run around in can make a dog more anxious because there's too much space for it to roam around and feel isolated in.

Additionally, if you're still house-training your Beagle, you definitely don't want to give her the freedom to use the potty wherever she pleases.

With the intactness of your home in mind, a good area to set your Beagle up to hang out in is a closed-off area such as a laundry room, bathroom, or gated-off hall.

Within this area, you want to ensure your dog has water, toys, and other things she enjoys that will make her comfortable. Toys should be interesting and interactive. If the toy requires a human presence to be fun, that toy will likely be ignored while your dog tries to dig her way to escape.

Another closed area to leave your pup is inside her crate. As mentioned before, crates can offer a sense of security to your Beagle, especially if you've spent time training your pup to be as comfortable as possible inside her crate.

A blanket tossed over most of the crate can make your Beagle feel like she's in a warm cave and can help lessen anxiety, but this isn't always the case. Some dogs may end up disliking their crate if they are left alone in it for too long, so know how long your pup can stand to be inside the crate before leaving her alone. Puppies can be crated for as long as their bladders hold.

To keep your Beagle occupied, consider purchasing a KONG dog toy or another chewable toy that can redirect her attention for a long period of time. Consider giving your pup a piece of clothing you're not concerned about ruining. Make sure it has your scent on it to make your pup feel less alone.

Dogs are creatures of habit and will sometimes start becoming anxious before you've even left the house because they recognize the signs of your getting ready. On days you don't have to leave the house, practice your leaving routine to get your dog used to the idea that you won't always leave. Once your pup realizes that your putting on your shoes isn't really a big deal, she'll be less anxious overall every time you do so, making her less anxious during moments when you have to leave her alone.

Along those same lines, when you leave and return home, don't make a big deal of greeting or saying goodbye to your dog. Doing so makes the act of your leaving and returning a big deal in your dog's mind when it should be an event that stimulates neither pleasure nor worry for your dog.

Overall, a good way to deal with separation anxiety is to just teach your pup to be alone, which won't be easy but will definitely save you and your Beagle long-term stress.

Similar to how I've outlined crate training, you want to have small blocks of time during which you leave your Beagle alone in part of your home while you are still home. Start with a few minutes at first, such as just going to the bathroom, and then work your way up to longer amounts of time leaving your dog alone: a 15-minute shower, 30-minute nap, 45-minute workout.

Build up your Beagle's tolerance to being alone, slowly, since pushing the limits of how long your pup can be alone can be counterproductive. Keep your ears open, and stay aware of if your dog is whining or panicking while alone during this training.

Running Away

Beagles are small and fast, which helps them track down and catch small game, but these traits also make it easy for them to escape unwary owners. The Beagle has been bred to listen to his nose, which tells him a lot of things about the world.

Beagles will often run away if they catch the scent of other dogs because Beagles want to hunt with other dogs. A Beagle will also just run away so he can explore the world without his owner pulling him away from a particularly interesting smell.

Don't feel betrayed by your Beagle, though. He isn't necessarily running away from you or from home but rather running toward something he really wants to investigate. Even though Beagles do have these strong urges to smell and track and run, you can still combat these urges to prevent your Beagle from running away.

To prevent running away at home, you can make sure your dog's outside area is secure. Just like with separation anxiety, if your dog is digging to escape, you can place large rocks or cement blocks around the bottom of the fence or dig down and place chicken wire at the base of the gate.

Another way Beagles may escape is by jumping over fences. Now, this one is unlikely to happen unless you've got some unwisely-placed furniture or storage in your backyard, but don't relax just because you think your Beagle won't utilize these escape tools. Beagles are great jumpers, and while they may be cautious and unsure of themselves at first, they will gain confidence to jump over higher and higher areas.

You can also monitor your Beagle and limit the amount of time he spends outside overall. Beagles are smart, so they may hide their escape activities for when they're alone, leaving their owners none-the-wiser about how their pup escaped.

For when you're outside, the most important thing to remember is not to unleash your dog. Keeping your Beagle on a leash trains him to stay close to you and not to roam far, an important method of training to help your Beagle control his urges and need to sniff. In fact, some trainers recommend leash training your Beagle for the first year—meaning when you're walking your pup, no matter how good he's been or how much he really wants to play with the neighborhood dogs, your Beagle should NOT be let off his leash. He may play for a few minutes but will eventually run away.

To get your pup to return to you after he's run away, make sure you've practiced the "Come" command with your dog. An untrained dog will not respect its owner and, therefore, will not come when called. Practice recall training with your pup to prevent a lost Beagle.

If your pup has escaped you, however he may have done it, and you can't find him, it's time to start searching. Beagles are good scent hounds and may be able to find their way home alone, but depending on how far their noses take them from home, you should be prepared to contact your local animal shelter, post a recent picture on social media pet- finder groups, and go out walking and calling your pup's name.

Bedtime

Although it may seem your dog will fall asleep literally anywhere, especially puppies, who may sleep around 18 hours a day, sleep is still as important for them as it is for a human, so having a comfortable place, or multiple comfortable places, set up around your home where your Beagle can sleep will make him much happier.

When dogs sleep in the wild, they do so in caves and dens that act as their nests, and you can duplicate the feeling of being inside a cave easily if you've purchased a crate for your Beagle. A blanket thrown over your pup's crate will create a cozy sleeping area for your Beagle.

A simple blanket is just the beginning, though. As your Beagle grows and develops favorite places, you'll find yourself finding creative nap areas.

I've gotten creative with giving Arthur multiple places to nap.

I've folded his crate blanket into thirds and placed it under my desk, placed the full blanket on the floor with all his toys on it to define a "play" area, created a crate "patio" by folding the blanket into a plush bed so Arthur can choose to sleep inside his open crate or outside of his crate but right next to the plush pillow placed on the inside of the crate (see how crate training can make training easier in other areas?), and I've even reused Amazon boxes and his folded blanket to create a pet bed.

As you can see, blankets, along with the couch, the carpet, your lap, your bed, his bed, everyone else's bed, and every other place he can reach, can easily be a great napping place for your pup and make bedtime a relaxing event wherein your dog feels at home in your home.

At night, and especially for anxious or destructive pups, crating is the best option. You can place your Beagle's crate anywhere it will fit, but beside your bed or in a central area of the house is best.

Many dog owners like to sleep with their pups in their rooms and in their beds. I've done so with Arthur, but he loves snuggling up with my partner at night who, sadly, isn't as fond as Arthur is about a nighttime pack pileup.

To be fair to Arthur, Beagles will do what they can to stay warm at night, so make sure that your Beagle has an appropriate AND acceptable sleep area.

If you're crating, your Beagle may cry at first at bedtime. If he's inside of a crate, even if that crate is in the middle of the family room with the rest of the pack around, your Beagle may cry to be let out to be closer to you.

Place the crate blanket over the top of the crate, turn off any lights that may be shining on the crate, and prepare to ignore the sad cries of your Beagle. Your Beagle will eventually quiet down and fall asleep, especially if you've taken him on a walk beforehand, ensured he's had dinner, and made sure he's gone potty. Puppy parenthood is a lot of work, but you're ready.

Leaving Your Dog Home Alone

Leaving your dog alone can instill you with guilt, especially when that dog is a Beagle who whines adorably and has a beautifully pleading expression. There's no reason to feel guilty for having to leaving your pup alone, though, as every dog should learn to be comfortable alone. Even though it's okay to leave your Beagle alone, you should still keep a few things in mind.

Don't leave your dog alone for more the eight hours at a time with food and water, and ideally no longer than four hours in general. If possible, hire a sitter or recruit a friend to come over to socialize your pup and let her out to relieve herself if you know you will be gone for a while.

Some dogs really don't mind being alone while others can't stand it and will develop separation anxiety which can result in destructive behavior and stress for you and your pup.

Besides crating your pup, a few things you can do to make leaving your dog alone less stressful is to play soothing dog music or TV for dogs. There are many YouTube videos created specifically for calming anxious dogs or that feature footage of wild animals in their natural habitats. Either is a good option to entertain your dog while you're away.

Additionally, if you're more worried about leaving your pup alone than she is about being alone, consider investing in security cameras that allow you to watch your pet while you're away, giving you peace of mind about the safety of your home and pet.

CHAPTER 6
House-Training

Different Options for Potty Training

If you've opted for a Beagle puppy, you're going to have to deal with house-training, and it is NOT fun. Even if your Beagle isn't a puppy, not all adult dogs are house-trained. Beagles can be naughty, intelligent, and lazy at the same time, so to avoid AVOIDABLE "accidents" in the house, start your Beagle's house-training by setting a schedule for your pup's potty time.

Puppies need to go to the bathroom eight to 10 times a day, and setting a potty schedule allows you to keep these bathroom times in appropriate areas as well as to organize other aspects of your pup's life. A schedule also saves you from a huge headache in the early days of your Beagle's training that is likely to stretch on through her life if uncorrected.

Set a house-training schedule that lets you allot some of your dog's potty times to walks, some to "after-dinner business meetings," and some to a brief playtime in the backyard before bed.

HELPFUL TIP
Consistency is Key

When house-training your dog, have the entire family use a single word or command to help your pet understand the importance of relieving himself outdoors. If you catch your dog in the act of relieving himself indoors, calmly say, "No," tuck his tail gently between his legs, pick him up, and take him outside immediately until he is successful. Praise him when he finishes. If you find that your dog has had an accident indoors, do not punish him. He will not understand the relationship between his prior accident and your scolding. Be patient and consistent while house-training your pet.

If your pup has unlimited access to water, you're going to be making a LOT of trips outside, so be warned. As Arthur came home at the end of a mild fall that introduced a very cold and very wet winter, we stayed inside a lot, and, unfortunately, Arthur grew to hate our trips outside.

If, for whatever reason, you and your pup decide that she can't make it outside (maybe you live on the top floor of an apartment and it's 3:00 a.m.?), having a backup plan is a must to keep your home clean and your puppy's training on track.

*Photo Courtesy of
Rachel Wilkins - picture by Rebecca Wuoti Photography*

Puppy pads are, of course, an easily-available option. Puppy pads can come as a combination of plastic, cloth, and paper; as a cut of fake plastic grass; or as a soft rubber grate that makes cleanup a snap,

Indoor dog toilets and dog litter boxes are also a thing, but since Arthur did so well with his house-training during the milder days of winter, I decided to incentivize him to go potty outside by putting his full-to-the-brim water bowl outside in the area we'd set up for him before he came home.

Most of Arthur and other puppies' accidents are pee accidents, so putting his water outside allowed me to predict when he'd need to pee next as well as to limit the amount of water he gulped down. Seriously, a Beagle will NOT stop drinking if it has free access to water. If you have cats, consider giving your Beagle and your cats their OWN bowls, and put both the water bowls and the food bowls somewhere your Beagle can't reach.

If, for some reason, you can't go outside while using this method (weather, injury, convenience, etc.), give your Beagle a small bowl of water inside. Eventually, she won't even think to go inside because she'll enjoy going outside to mark her territory.

As for poos, well, a puppy will poo 10 to 60 minutes after eating, so you should be able to control and limit those with careful attention to your dog's habits and training schedule.

The First Few Weeks

"Puppies are most likely to use the bathroom within 15 minutes of eating, drinking, playing, exercising or waking up from a nap. After any of these activities your puppy should be given the opportunity to go to the bathroom."

Chey Ballard
Rajun Cajun Kennels

As I mentioned, a schedule for house-training your Beagle will help her succeed in not ruining your carpets or leaving an inescapable smell in your hallways. Dogs thrive on consistency both scheduling-wise as well as location-wise. Same time, same place every day for the first month or two, and your pup will have no trouble relieving herself where she's supposed to.

Slowly acclimating your new Beagle to new areas can help reduce accidents. You won't always be around to help your pup not potty inside, so consider leaving your pup in a small area where she can comfortably walk around. Her crate is the obvious choice. As we've already discussed, your Beagle's crate should be her safe place, and she'll want to keep it smelling like her and not her waste.

Photo Courtesy of Scott Runge

Staying consistent with the time and location of potty time will keep waste contained to one area of your property. Remember that your puppy has a small bladder, and accidents that she makes will usually be your fault for not taking her out. She doesn't yet know that there are areas that she isn't allowed to relieve herself, and it's your job to consistently show her where she can go to the bathroom.

Imagine if you couldn't tell the difference between signs on bathrooms in public. Where would you go? Your pup will relieve herself where she can and will usually try to go out of the public area to do so.

*Photo Courtesy of
Miranda Schmitter*

HELPFUL TIP
House-Training

Beagles have the reputation of being somewhat difficult to house-train. Be diligent and consistent while training your pet. To avoid accidents in the house, owners should consider crate training their pet. The crate should only be large enough for the dog to get up and turn around while inside the crate. Since dogs do not like to soil their beds, crate training is advisable. Whenever you are not home with your pet, or at night, he should be crated. The crate is not a punishment, but is similar to a den, making your dog feel safe and comfortable.

An important fact to remember is that a dog will avoid soiling an area that it considers to be its home, play, or living area. You may notice that your dog will walk off a bit into the grass before relieving herself, even in the backyard. If you make your pup feel at home in every part of your home she's allowed (slowly, and one area at a time!), she will be even more reluctant to make a mess inside.

Again, you need to guide your pup to the appropriate areas when it's potty time, so letting your Beagle know when it's potty time should be your top priority. Understand when your Beagle needs to relieve herself (usually after waking up, eating, drinking, and playing), and plan your house-training schedule accordingly.

And remember, with all your Beagle training, praise good behavior with treats, attention, and toys. Rewarding positive behavior will ensure you continue to see that behavior.

Playpens and Doggy Doors

Playpens, doggy doors, and other barriers are a must when you live with a Beagle. This doesn't apply just to puppies: Beagles of any age will curiously explore any area and get into any mess they find.

A doggy door will keep your Beagle inside when you don't want him going out, maybe because of bad weather or because it's bedtime. A doggy door will also prevent pests from entering your home if your solution to giving your pup access to the backyard so far has been leaving the backdoor open (which I am guilty of).

Aim for a sturdy doggy door when you're searching. Doggy doors can be as high as $400 or as low as $30, depending on how heavy-duty you need your dog's door to be. Installation is another cost to consider if you're not confident that you can do the installation yourself or you lack the tools. Search for services or check with local pet stores for installation availability.

You may need to block your pet from entering an area of the house during house-cleaning times, when a maintenance person is working in or outside your home, or maybe just when your pup is being bothersome to the family and other pets.

For playpens, consider the needs of your pets as well as your available space. There are some playpens that come attached to crates, so if you have multiple pets, that might be an option, but for a Beagle, you don't need to get too huge with a playpen. In fact, a simple baby gate and a hazard-free area is a simple solution to the playpen problem.

Photo Courtesy of Heather Voelker

If you don't have a playpen or a baby gate, you can create your own doggy barrier. I think I mentioned before that Beagles are good jumpers. Do believe me when I say this: your makeshift playpen needs to be high enough to prevent your Beagle from jumping over it. It should also leave no cracks on either side of the barrier because your Beagle will squeeze through.

With a doggy door, playpen, baby gate, or DIY barrier, you can keep your pup out of trouble.

CHAPTER 7
Socializing With People and Animals

Beagles are naturally social dogs. They were bred to hunt in a 'pack'. They actually do better if they are around other animals. It can be another dog or even a cat."

Carolyn Miller
GEM Beagles

Importance of Good Socialization

Beagles go through a lot of critical stages in their mental and physical growth, especially early on. One important area of growth to pay attention to is socialization. Socialization is important for healthy psychological growth. From ages 8-16 weeks is an especially vital time. Dogs who are socialized early on have better coping skills, adjust well to new or strange situations and places, and play better with other animals.

HELPFUL TIP
Pack-Dog Mentality

You should begin socializing your Beagle at between 7-14 weeks of age. Since the Beagle is a pack dog, he will crave attention and the company of other dogs and people. Your dog is social by nature and will do well around other dogs. Your scrappy little Beagle should be kept away from bigger dog breeds, however, until he is fully socialized. He may get into tussles with larger dogs, so be on the lookout for this type of behavior. Check the internet for Beagle socializing clubs in your area.

Socialization of a dog comes in many forms that contribute to its overall happiness and mental health. Socialization with dogs comes in the form of playing with humans and other animals, meaning you and your family should be playing with your new Beagle regularly to keep him entertained and introducing him to a variety of people. Besides, who would want to sit around in a boring house or bare backyard with nothing to do and no one to play with? Explore with your pup and meet new people!

Photo Courtesy of
Steven Kent

Beagles should explore textures, sounds, locations, and heights.

Give your Beagle all kinds of toys to chew on such as toys made of wood, bumpy plastic, rough plastic, treats, or other pet-safe materials. Doing so will help prevent your Beagle from chewing things he's not supposed to be chewing on.

Chew toys and other toys that make a lot of interesting sounds are also popular socialization options. Your Beagle will love to hold a squeaky toy in his mouth and squeeze it over and over.

Placing chairs, small blocks, raised planks, ramps, and other obstacles around your yard can provide your Beagle with a lot of obstacles to run and jump around to show off his skills. If you have other pets or host puppy playdates, your backyard will be popular with other animals, giving your Beagle another level of socialization by allowing him to be around his friends during playtime.

Proper socialization eliminates fear and aggressive behaviors such as barking and growling at other dogs who may be bigger or smaller, growling at people in a specific uniform or who wear hats or jackets. You want a calm dog when you're getting your mail delivered or when you take your Beagle to the vet.

Just think about the fact that your pup sees in a limited spectrum of colors, and most of the time, he sees you inside your home wearing regular clothes. Many uniforms are in colors a dog can see and also have parts of a uniform that you don't normally have attached to you.

Your Beagle likely won't know what to think and will react to protect himself and, as is often the case, other members of the pack. It's your job to introduce your pup to a spectrum of people early on.

Most importantly, you want your Beagle to be properly socialized around other dogs because dogs can often be unpredictable, and you, at least, should be able to predict what your dog will do based on what you train him to do.

So, start off good socialization with a well-trained Beagle. If things get out of hand, you'll want to be able to get your pup out of the situation with a single command. Beagles are stubborn, so you must work hard at training your Beagle to obey you.

Beagles can sometimes antagonize other dogs, no matter their size. It comes with the breed, but can be an occupational hazard at the dog park when a larger dog doesn't take well to your dog's antics.

As you already know, your Beagle loves to be around you, your family, and other animals. It's just in their nature to be pack dogs, more so even than other dogs. If you don't have other pets, though, properly socializing your dog with other animals may be hard, and even when you have other pets, your dogs should be meeting as many dogs as possible early on in his life.

Your Beagle should start socializing with other dogs and people around the time you begin training. Beagles are naturally playful, but an unsocialized Beagle can be aggressive. They also have a tendency to chance cats, and while that behavior may seem okay to your own cats if you have them, other cats will not appreciate a strange dog chasing them. Teach your Beagle not to chase cats!

You want your Beagle to be confident, but you also want him to be calm. There are plenty of opportunities for socialization such as with other pet owners in your neighborhood (there are apps you can connect with them through), your friends' pets, at a dog park, or by dog sitting (an opportunity to earn extra money as well).

Arthur and I host other dogs in the neighborhood and walk them during the day sometimes. Many people don't have time to walk their

dogs during the day while they're away, but as a Beagle owner, you're more likely to be home and may have the opportunity to help out (I suggest one dog at a time, though, as Beagles can easily get out of hand and be excited around other dogs).

There are also socializing clubs. Look around your area for availability. Some clubs are even breed-specific, and since Beagles are one of the most popular dog breeds in America, you're likely to find a club where you can socialize your Beagle.

It's not just dangers from other dogs that you want to be aware of. Beagles can be annoying and may antagonize other dogs. You want your dog to be polite. Think about how annoying and painful it is to be greeted by an excited dog with sharp nails. Dogs, again, especially Beagles, will stand and lean against people's legs to sniff or out of excitement. This behavior can be dangerous to older people, people with disabilities, or children.

Along with socializing with other animals, your Beagle should be socializing with humans other than you and your family. The Beagle needs to be socialized often and from a young age to be cooperative with children, people, and other animals.

Don't automatically assume that because your puppy loves your children, he will love all children as he grows or that he will be safe to leave alone around other children.

When meeting new people in public, keep your Beagle on his leash within a five to six-foot range of you. It's also smart to keep treats with you because Beagles respond best to food.

If your pup hasn't met someone yet, let them offer him a treat and tell him to sit for more treats. He'll soon learn that strangers are just as friendly as everyone at home is.

If your Beagle shows signs of aggression, move away from the stranger and the situation. Don't force friendships with new people or new dogs. Not every dog will like every other dog, and you may end up exacerbating some underlying issue.

If you know that there are a few people you want to introduce your pup to, set up the introduction and plan what will happen. Play with your pup beforehand to get him relaxed and in a good mood and to create a positive association with visitors.

Whether you're introducing your Beagle to people at home or while on the go, make sure that you stay calm so that you can control the situ-

ation. Watch for how your dog is reacting to people, and know when it's time to step in and help.

Take your Beagle to as many new places as possible. This may mean that you must go on new adventures too, but it's your responsibility to make sure to socialize your Beagle and expose him to new experiences.

Overall, Beagles have a good temperament and are usually good with children and other dogs. While they may make some scary noises while trying to get others to play, a well-trained and properly-socialized Beagle will be kind and safe to play with.

Since Beagles love lots of attention and lots of exercise, you can take your Beagle with you to family reunions or other places there may be children. As long as you're keep a close eye, you can rest easy knowing that a trained Beagle will happily and cheerfully play well with children.

CHAPTER 8
Beagles and Your Other Pets

"Beagles are considered social pack dogs. To them the more animals the merrier! So it is no problem to bring a beagle home to other pets (even an adult Beagle is thrilled to meet new friends). However, your current pet may not be as thrilled, so take it slow. After about a week most dogs with adjust and start to bond. Cats can take much longer, but they too eventually adjust to their new Beagle friend."

Linda Tordai
TheBeagleBarn.com

*Photo Courtesy of
Michelle Zfira*

Introducing Your New Puppy to Other Animals

Whether you're introducing your new Beagle to your other dogs or introducing them to a new playmate, it's important for you, as the owner and trainer of your Beagle, to first understand not only pack mentality but also how to properly introduce dogs to each other or to other pets. Remember that as the human, you are the translator. Not all dogs will understand and like each other, and most cats definitely don't understand that sometimes a Beagle is howling because he doesn't know how else to get them to play.

HELPFUL TIP
Companionship

Although your Beagle is a pack dog that seeks companionship, introduce him gently and safely to other animals. He may need some assistance while learning the difference between expected behaviors and natural behaviors. Look for safe places to offer interaction with other dogs while training and socializing your Beagle. Be cautious when introducing him to new pets.

Of course, this is where proper socialization comes in.

The first time you introduce your Beagle to your other pets, you want them to be in different rooms, divided by a door. They'll get used to each others' smell eventually, especially if you give them toys to play with and then exchange those toys.

Your current pets may not be as excited for the new dog as you are, so keep that in mind and respect the current workings of the house. Introducing new pets is a process, so take the time to make a plan to make that process run smoothly and safely.

Note that cats do not easily get along with dogs, especially if they aren't used to dogs, and small dogs such as Beagles can be annoying to any other animal because of their energy level and tendency to run about.

Introduce only one pet at a time in a small room, take things slowly, and keep all introductions supervised. It's important for you to be paying attention to the nonverbal behaviors and cues from both of your pets in this moment.

Outside of meeting your own pets, when you introduce a dog to another dog, those who have had more socialization usually do better and have fewer problems socializing. This bravery with socializing may turn off shyer dogs.

*Photo Courtesy of
Isobel Gee*

CHAPTER 8 Beagles and Your Other Pets

Dogs who aren't spayed or neutered are also likely to be more excitable and may lead to a more difficult first introduction.

Start off your Beagle's introduction to a new dog by starting in neutral place such as outside in the front yard or on the street or at the park (but not a park your dog is familiar with unless it's a dog park). It depends on if your dog considers that place his territory if the new dog is coming to your home. A good way to prevent your dog from being over-territorial is to control where he does his business. The front yard can easily stay neutral if your pup isn't allowed to roam free to mark it.

When introducing new dogs, make sure both are leashed for the safety of everyone involved. The adults holding the leashes should be calm and should have practiced commands with the dogs.

Keep the leashes free of tension as the dogs are likely to already be tense and anxious themselves.

Give the dogs treats away from each other to associate the situation with pleasurable things, then allow the dogs to slowly sniff each other in greeting. Keep watch for aggressive stances, behaviors, growls, or barks.

Dogs respond well to verbal feedback given by humans, so if things are really getting tense, speak in a soothing voice to your pup and have the other owner do the same. They should calm down and then maybe you can offer them a new chance to introduce themselves to each other.

Behavior to watch out for:

- Stiff bodies, especially if there is eye contact and raised hair. Dogs may bare their teeth, and if so, you'll know these two aren't going to get along easily.

- Overly-excited meetings may make some dogs react fearfully. Keep your dog controlled either way. Don't let him rush up into someone else's personal space, especially when that someone is a strange.

- Playfulness can easily turn bad if one dog ignores the warnings another gives. Step in if you see that your dog is the one provoking others. Beagles do have a tendency to be annoying if they aren't getting the attention they feel they deserve.

Pack Mentality

Photo Courtesy of Donna Shipway

Pack mentality is something that humans and dogs both practice. It refers to the social hierarchy that wolves in the wild live by, though it isn't exactly clear how much dogs hold by the same instincts. Wild wolf packs are led by a mating mother and father, with the rest of the pack being their children from recent years.

There is a pecking order within a pack, and in a household, a human should be the pack leader. In a home with multiple dogs, there may be one dog who is naturally the leader among all of the dogs, but a human should be the natural alpha of them all.

When you bring a new dog home, it's important to establish yourself as the pack leader. You can do this by setting rules for your dog to abide by as well as showing your dog the consequences for breaking these rules. Establishing yourself as alpha can be as simple as completing your dog's training and being consistent with showing who's in control.

Sometimes, the dog social hierarchy can lead to fighting amongst your dogs. Tension between dogs can arise for many a reason, and while Beagles are friendly dogs, they can also be jealous or provoke others.

Since anything can cause two dogs to start fighting, it's important to identify the triggering stressors if you find yourself with two fighting dogs. Fighting can occur because of possessive aggression, territorial aggression, fear aggression, defensive aggression, and more.

Figure out where your dog is aiming her aggression to figure out which stressor is to blame. Maybe your pup feels cornered or trapped, or maybe she feels as if someone is taking a precious toy of hers. Determining the source of the stressor can help you understand the behavior.

Unfortunately, there are times when you can't handle your dog's bad behavior on your own. Aggression can lead to fighting, dog attacks, and destructive behavior.

If your dog has become unruly or doesn't get along with your other pets, consider hiring a professional dog trainer. Dog trainers deal with an array of behavioral issues, and a dog behavioralist will more specifically know how to keep the peace in your home.

You can try to keep both your new pet and your old pet separated, but you will have to keep an eye on them at all times, and even then, you may have trouble with fighting.

If behavioral training either isn't an option or doesn't work, consider rehoming your dog. Many people are looking specifically for Beagles, so you can connect with those looking to adopt to find a right fit if that fit isn't with you.

Consider options like the Humane Society or other no-kill shelters. These places also sometimes have foster programs that can further help socialize the Beagle if you have to give him up. Rehoming can be a good thing for your Beagle as well, who will definitely be happy in a forever home where he fits in.

Additionally, if you bought your Beagle from a responsible breeder, he or she will take back any of the puppies adopted from them.

CHAPTER 9
Physical and Mental Exercise

"All Beagles should have playtime and exercise time. A new puppy should be taken out for exercise and play at least every 3 hours. Your adult dog should be let out in the yard or walked at least 3-4 times a day. Beagles are versatile; they love activity just as much as they love lying on the couch. This makes them so easy to adjust to any family's life style."

Linda Tordai
TheBeagleBarn.com

*Photo Courtesy of
Terry & Lydia Donner*

Exercise Requirements

Your Beagle, like you, requires daily exercise. Your Beagle should receive a mix of moderate and more intensive exercise. Walks at least one to two times a day are a must for Beagles and are the least that should be available. More intensive exercises may include playing fetch or going for a run at least one to three times a week. Don't forget about your Beagle's tiny legs! Though they have a lot of energy, make sure whatever exercise you engage your Beagle in is appropriate for her.

Your Beagle needs to stretch her muscles to keep them healthy and working properly, and this is one reason not to leave your pup in her crate for too long. Proper exercise helps to main your Beagle's muscle mass as well as keeping her metabolism working as it should. The biggest benefit to proper exercise, of course, is having a worn-out Beagle. Trust me, these long winter days have had me planning a lot of outdoor activities for Arthur this spring.

Long walks are the simplest exercise you can engage your dog in. Walking for a long time shouldn't be too much of a problem for your Beagle, whose ancestors used to run for miles at a time.

HELPFUL TIP
Let's Get Physical

Beagles need moderate exercise; long walks, several times a day, as puppies are suggested. He will be healthier if allowed and encouraged to take part in cardiovascular activity. Short bursts of activity, such as chasing after a ball or fetching a stick, will encourage well-being. While these activities are encouraged, do not pull items from your dog's mouth. Instead, teach your Beagle to "drop" items on your command. This will aid in avoiding aggressive behavior such as nipping and growling.

Runs are next on the list and require more effort on your part but provide great exercise for both you and your Beagle. Running will also tire your Beagle out much quicker than walking will and may help burn off some extra calories your Beagle may have snuck while you weren't watching.

Bike riding is a fun option, especially if you need to run to the store and you're environmentally conscious. It's vital that you purchase a leash bike attachment made specifically for walking your dog while biking. Failing to do so may result in serious injuries to you or to your dog.

Hiking is another option and one dog owners may love as well. Hiking doesn't have to be insanely time-consuming or energy-consuming. Many cities have short local hiking trails where you can take your Beagle. A hike is a good way to simulate the environment your Beagle's ancestors grew up. Ending your excursion at a dog park or other playtime-acceptable area is sure to leave you with a worn-out pup. This tip is good to remember if you're having a lot of guests over who may excite your Beagle to the point of forgetting her training.

Playing fetch is a classic and can be done with almost anything, although you should be careful of giving your Beagle anything harmful to her teeth. Throwing toys may tire your arm out in the long run, but it will also tire your Beagle's tiny body out in the process. Eventually, your Beagle will get tired of bringing her toys back to you and will run off to chew one to pieces, leaving you free to rest.

Create your own agility or dog show at home if your pup doesn't compete. Your pup will enjoy running around the obstacles you place for her, and you'll enjoy watching her show off the beauty of the Beagle breed. You can make ramps, use parking cones, utilize wheels as hurdles, and place tunnels around for your dog. She'll be entertained for a long time with such a playground in her backyard.

Of course, physical exercise isn't the only exercise your Beagle needs. Mental exercises are important to maintain the edge of your Beagle's in-

Photo Courtesy of Beth Forbey

Photo Courtesy of Christian Lechner

tellect, and exercises that make your dog think, such as agility shows are great for making your dog think. An agility course is both a physical and mental challenge for your Beagle and doesn't have to be expensive to create and maintain.

Another option for mental exercise is hiding your Beagle's favorite thing around the house: food. Give your Beagle a hint of what hunting out prey feels like by allowing her to find her favorite treats under blankets or behind furniture. She'll spend a lot of time sniffing every corner to make sure no treat went uneaten.

Mental exercise may not be on the top list for you when it comes to your dog, but stimulating your Beagle's mind can truly bring out the best in her. Intellectual stimulation for your dog can enrich her life as well as deepen your bond with her since this stimulation comes via playtime. Mental stimulation also allows you another opportunity to train your pup to be polite and well-rounded.

There really is no wrong way to play with your dog, and many exercises involve both your dog's body as well as her mind. Along with the usual exercises to do with your dog, consider the following:

- Create a doggy scavenger hunt using toys and, most importantly, treats! Follow your dog around and have him solve challenges to get the next prize. Challenges can be as simple as sitting and staying successfully or completing a complicated maneuver.

Photo Courtesy of Samantha Harley

- Utilize cardboard boxes to make forts and obstacle courses. Hide treats and toys throughout.

- Pretend to be a dog. If your dog is the only dog in your house, she'll especially find it interesting that you're acting like her. She'll turn her head to one side right before she tries convincing you to play.

- Play hide-and-seek! Hide somewhere in your home and call your Beagle. Try quietly moving to a new hiding spot without your Beagle noticing. Keep it up as long as possible, and up the stakes by hiding with snacks ready to be given out.

- Do magic tricks. Your Beagle is just a tiny two-year-old, so she'll be fascinated and awed if you walk behind a blanket, only to have disappeared when the blanket falls away. Learn some new skills, and teach your Beagle a thing or two about magic.

Photo Courtesy of Scott Mamone

- Be creative! Playing with your dog is not brain science. She will find anything to entertain themselves, so anything you do with her will be a treat. Just make sure you and your Beagle stay safe during playtime!

CHAPTER 10
Training your Beagle

"Beagles are a smart breed. Often people confuse their tenacious determination with lack of intelligence. This is not the case."

Dennis Dollar
Barrister Beagles

Clear Expectations

Photo Courtesy of
Ma. Kristine Basco

While Beagles are the epitome of "man's best friend," they are also stubbornly independent dogs that often require food to convince them to take any action they didn't think of themselves. Beagles can be such great pets to have around while also having little inclination to please their owners, but a well-trained Beagle will definitely respect you enough to follow your commands more often than not.

I say more often than not rather than "always" because your Beagle will not always listen to you. Beagles are easily distracted by food, random smells, other dogs, new people, strange sounds, movement in the distance ... you get the idea. Anything that CAN distract your Beagle WILL distract your Beagle.

It's a challenge to get a Beagle to do what you want because they are so easily distracted. Even at home, you might find your Beagle moving, looking, and sniffing around instead of paying attention to you.

Training will help your Beagle curb his urges and control himself better as well as get him used to listening to your commands. Training allows you to practice getting your Beagle's attention. When your Beagle focuses on something, he's focused, and if that subject of his focus tempts him enough, you'll want to know that your dog will obey you when you tell him to stop.

Truly, an untrained dog, no matter the breed, can be annoying and dangerous. Beagles enjoy chewing, but their baby teeth will fall out eventually to be replaced with adult chewing. Training early prevents unfortunate incidents as well as destroyed property. Training can help with so many behaviors and really isn't time-consuming over the course of your dog's life.

And finally, spending time training your Beagle deepens the connection the two of you have together. Training is an act of communication and understanding between you and your Beagle. While it definitely takes some time and patience in the first few months, consistency and dedication to your Beagle's training results in a well-behaved Beagle who will enrich the lives of your family for years to come.

Operant Conditioning Basics

Operant conditioning is a scientific principle that allows you to create an association for your dog between a behavior and either a consequence or a reward for that behavior. Operant conditioning is a method of training sometimes used in the study of lab rats, but this training

Photo Courtesy of
Alayne Rae Mullen
Lane Rae Kennels

method also plays a part in the everyday learning of people and animals around the world. This type of training or learning is used to change old behaviors and to instill new ones.

So what does this information mean for how you can train your Beagle? Well, think of it this way: If you praise your Beagle every time he sits when you command him to, he'll be more likely to sit next time you tell him to, even if no praise follows the next instance of his sitting. If you consistently praise your dog for positive behavior, he will associate being obedient and polite with positive feelings because you are strengthening your dog's association of obedience and positivity.

Conversely, associating negative behavior with a scolding or punishment will make your Beagle less likely to perform that action in the future because he knows by taking that negative action, he will experience an unpleasant outcome.

Basically, operant condition is any behavior that has been influenced by training, and there are four areas to keep in mind for successfully understanding your dog's behavior as well as your response to that behavior:

Photo Courtesy of
Jena Mobley

Photo Courtesy of Danny Put

Positive: The dog's behavior makes something be added.

Negative: The dog's behavior makes something be taken away.

Reinforcement: The behavior increases or is strengthened.

Punishment: The behavior is decreased or extinguished.

The positive and negatives can be combined with the reinforcement and the punishment, depending on the situation.

Positive Reinforcement	Your dog sits, and you give him a treat.
Negative Reinforcement	Your dog sits after you push his butt down.
Positive Punishment	Your dog jumps on you, and you yell at him.
Negative Punishment	Your dog jumps on you, and you turn your back to him and ignore him.

Truly, operant conditioning works on humans, dogs, and other animals. Your Beagle is smart enough to learn as long as you are consistently teaching him. Reinforcement is used much more often than punishment and works better and more consistently in the long run.

Primary Reinforcements

"Beagles think for themselves. They were bred to hunt independently from their owner, so you have to convince them to do something. The best way to do that is with food. They will do anything for a treat. Just be careful that they don't get 'pudgy' from all the treats you give them."

Carolyn Miller
GEM Beagles

Primary reinforcements do not require learning in order for your dog to understand that he enjoys these things, and they are the easiest reinforcements to use when training your dog simply for the fact that your dog wants and needs these things already. Some reinforcements may work better than others, depending on your dog's preferences.

Primary reinforcements to use when training your Beagle include food, water, praise, treats, and anything else he already enjoys. Simply encourage the behavior you want to continue seeing by, for example, praising your pup when he returns from peeing outside, giving him his food bowl after telling him to sit, practicing "sit" and "stay" during playtime and rewarding with more playtime and more.

You can see how these primary reinforcements so easily work for training. Eventually, you'll find more specific things that your Beagle likes more than others, but remember that your Beagle is not going to stop wanting your attention, and he's not going to stop liking food, so these reinforcements are tools you can use consistently to encourage the behavior you want to see.

Secondary Reinforcements

A secondary reinforcement lets your dog know that a primary reinforcement is incoming. Secondary reinforcements include verbal commands, hand signals, or the sound of a clicker or other training tool. Secondary reinforcements are exactly what they're described as: a second pleasurable or memorable thing your dog can recognize as connected with a certain behavior he's performed and/or an action you want him to take.

Secondary reinforcements should be reinforced with primary reinforcements, and while you can use secondary reinforcements without primary ones, you should continue to associate the primary reinforcement in your dog's mind with the secondary one.

Photo Courtesy of Monika Barany

A secondary reinforcement is something such as a dog toy. Your dog wasn't born knowing what, say, a ball is, but he eventually learns that a ball can be used for fun. When you're rewarding your dog with playtime, his favorite ball acts as a secondary reinforcement.

Secondary reinforcements are not replacements for primary reinforcements. They are additional indications to your dog that they are correctly following their training and are intended to offer your dog more of a reason to be obedient. Since Beagles can be very stubborn, this type of training is highly recommended for a consistently well-behaved dog. Regular use of secondary reinforcement is important for it to keep working for your dog.

Dangers of Negative Reinforcement, Correction, Punishment After the Fact

HELPFUL TIP
Stop Whining!

You will begin to recognize several different "whines" coming from your Beagle. Listen for the difference between the "I need to go outside" whine, the "I'm hungry" howl, and the tone of "I just want attention" whining. Until you learn and can distinguish these whines, check on your Beagle to see what might be the cause of his whining. Always ignore nighttime whining. If you pay attention to this type of unwanted complaint from your dog, you will be encouraging the poor behavior. Some pet owners use a metal can or box with coins placed inside to provide reinforcement when their dog is whining. By shaking the can or box of coins, the dog associates the annoying noise with the unwanted behavior. Be consistent with your pet. You'll be glad you did.

You can easily make your Beagle afraid and confused if you misunderstand the meaning and use of negative reinforcement. Negative reinforcement is the act of taking something away from your dog to encourage a specific behavior, but many people interpret negative reinforcement as a punishment for their dogs.

Negative reinforcement can be used to shape behavior. By removing something pleasant from your dog's life as a result of unpleasant behavior, you are encouraging a certain behavior, but many people use tactics such as kicking, hitting, or otherwise punishing their dogs to get them to understand that their behavior is unacceptable.

These punishments can be dangerous and may make your dog defensive. These tactics also teach your dog to be aggressive. Additionally, when you're training your dog, you're also training yourself, and you do not want to train yourself that hitting and kicking your dog is a good way to get your way. Training can be frustrating, and in a particularly tense moment, you don't want to be using punishing tactics to correct your dog's behavior.

Some punishments can make dogs fearful and anxious, so even if they do not become aggressive, they are suffering, and so is your relationship with them. You don't want your dog to associate you with fear, and while he may not become aggressive immediately, he may do so later. Dogs may even become aggressive toward the source of the punishment such as newspapers or brooms, resulting in destruction and possible injury.

Other dangers that come along with training include delayed and inconsistent punishments. Your dog's behavior should be corrected in the moment that behavior is happening. Your dog will not understand if you punish him for something he did five minutes ago because five minutes is a long time to a dog, and he likely doesn't remember he did something bad.

Additionally, not correcting a specific behavior every time will make your dog think that behavior is okay sometimes and can also make your commands less effective as your dog learns to ignore them.

Obedience is something all dogs need to learn, and you, as the owner, are responsible for ensuring your dog is properly trained.

Training can happen anywhere. You can learn from a book, from YouTube, from a class, or even just hire a trainer to train your dog for you.

A trainer will definitely give you faster and more consistent results compared to DIY training, simply because of the fact that trainers are trained to train. Training your dog yourself can take a lot of time, and while you may be planning to spend lots of time with your Beagle regardless, not everyone has unlimited time to allocate to training.

New dog owners also suffer from inconsistency, lack of clarity, and lack of firmness. It's important to remember that your dog isn't human, so you need to make what you want your dog to do as clear as possible. Many people fail to be clear and consistent, teaching their dog that they don't have anything of value to say. They also fail to follow through on training with their dogs because of pleading expressions. As a Beagle owner, you should harden yourself to cute looks as soon as possible.

A trainer will be consistent with lessons and will teach those lessons professionally. A trainer has experience communicating with dogs and knows how to be as clear as possible. A trainer sees many adorable dogs,

Photo Courtesy of
Victoria Malova

so your Beagle's cute face will not convince the trainer that he doesn't have to follow directions.

A trainer is also obviously going to cost more than YouTube videos or books, but a trainer will have more experience with handling and teaching a dog in a shorter amount of time. A trainer also allows you to spend more quality time with your dog, free from the frustrations involved in the training process, because trust me, it is frustrating to train an independent creature who doesn't speak the same language as you.

On the other hand, attending a class, especially if you're a new dog owner, teaches owners many vital lessons as well as deepening the bond between you and the dog. Classes offer your dog a chance to socialize with other dogs, which is important for the first few months of a dog's life.

Obedience classes will likely be cheaper than hiring a trainer since the trainer isn't working one-on-one with your dogs, and you will get hands-on knowledge about how to handle your dog day-to-day; however, a trainer will not be with you after your dog's training is over. These classes give you an opportunity to see how other owners handle their dogs and let you see that your dog may not be the most misbehaved of the lot.

Remember that behavioral training is for both you AND your dog. Don't expect that your dog is the only one who needs to learn how things should go. It's your job to show your dog the correct way to live, and you can only do that by first knowing yourself, then by learning how to correct your dog in a way that he understands.

Overall, remember that your dog's behavior is inherently linked to your behavior. Most dogs aren't hard to train and are eager to receive attention from their owners, but daily reinforcement of these commands in your dog's day-to-day life are what will ensure that your dog remains well-trained. That means that you have to remember that your dog isn't allowed on the couch so that you can tell him "down." Even if he's learned before that he's not allowed there, you must remind him.

Behavioral problems are the top reason dogs end up in shelters. It's not fair for a dog not to have a home because its owners did not hold themselves to the same training standards they hold their dog to, so make sure that you remain motivated to maintain your dog's training throughout his life.

CHAPTER 11
Basic Commands

"It's always play time with Beagles. They love to play 24 hours a day, 365 days a year."

Chey Ballard
Rajun Cajun Kennels

Benefits of Proper Training

Training your dog to learn some basic commands is important for developing a healthy relationship with your dog, and more than just puppies need to learn proper training. You and your Beagle don't speak the same language, but training allows you to teach your dog some simple commands that help you to guide its behavior to be more aligned with the behavior of your Beagle's new pack.

Dogs look to their pack mates to determine how they should behave, and as humans, we certainly have different rules for how to behave compared to packs of dogs. It's our job to educate our dogs. Obedience training eliminates stress for you and your dog as well as making your dog overall happier and more self-confident.

Teaching your dog even basic commands can make managing your Beagle so much easier. There are many situations pet owners will go through that they aren't aware that they need to be prepared for, and practicing commands such as stop, drop, and sit could potentially save your Beagle's life.

You may need to use commands at home, outside on a walk, or out in public around other dogs. You really can't predict when your dog will get into trouble or get out of your control momentarily.

Learning commands also makes your dog perfect for dog-friendly areas. Untrained dogs don't do well there because they may get excited or nervous around other dogs and may become otherwise uncontrollable.

Additionally, if your dog gets away from you in public out of excitement or fear, you want to be able to call her back and be fairly confident she'll listen.

Picking the Right Rewards/Treats

Proper training doesn't happen right away and can even be hard to start off with if you don't have the proper incentives. There are lots of ways you can reward your dog for doing a good job or for completing a task. Remember, though, that rewards are not bribes! Your dog should learn the reward after having completed the task, and you should not wave the reward in front of her to convince her to complete the task.

Photo Courtesy of Niki Medina

Some rewards commonly used in dog training include treats, playtime, toys, warm words, and warm touches. Which rewards work best really depend on what the dog prioritizes as good, fun, or desirable. Some rewards also work better depending on the situation or the skill/behavior being taught. Overall, you don't want to rely on one reward for your dog because there can be too much of a good thing. Mix up rewards to keep your dog interested in being obedient.

Most dog owners should be careful about over-relying on treats as a reward since your dog can easily just see you as a treat dispenser, but as I've already mentioned, treats are a must when training Beagles. They are stubborn and don't respond to much else.

Since you likely know you'll be using treats in your training, it's still important to know what kind of treats work for training. There are two distinctions to make with treats for training: fast-eating treats and slow-eating treats.

Slow-eating treats are important but aren't going to be your primary treats while training. Slow-eating treats, since they last so long, are good for training your dog to sit quietly, to enjoy her crate, or to simply pass the time without excessive energy. Such treats include rawhide treats, bones, KONG toys, bully sticks, and anything else that takes your dog more than a bite or two to eat.

Fast-eating treats are things your dog can eat in one or two bites without distracting her from the training at hand. They're usually small and soft and come in a bag with lots of similar treats, which is convenient for repetitively training one skill, over and over. Crunchier treats or bigger treats are okay but can be more distracting to your dog because they make more crumbs she has to search for and take longer to eat.

Training Methods

Photo Courtesy of Karla Greer

There are as many ways to train a dog as there are dog owners in the world, and even professional dog trainers often disagree about which methods work, which are ethical, and which should be left in the past of behavioral training.

I do want to say that none of these methods of training are more correct than any other. I, personally, rely on "relationship-based training" which somewhat combines several training methods I'll discuss. I have friends who choose to train their dogs with the dominance method, and when we do doggy playdates, I can see some of my own methods within his.

Whichever training method you choose, what matters, in the end, is that you and your dog bond in the process of training his obedience.

Common Training Methods

- Positive Reinforcement Training

This is the type of training discussed in Chapter 10 and the one we recommend. The thought behind this training method is that dogs will continue repeating a behavior when that behavior is reinforced with something the dog wants such as treats or toys. This method of training requires consistency and for every member of the household to know the rules and rewards system.

- Dominance Training

Dominance training is based on outdated research about the workings of wolf packs, but it's still a popular method of dog training today. This method of training relies on a dog's instinctual needs to be part of a pack and to know his place within the pack. Training with this method requires that the owner make him or herself known as the alpha so that the dog will respect and listen to them.

- Clicker Training

Clicker training, similar to positive reinforcement training, uses the concepts of operant conditioning. While using a clicker is listed as a secondary reinforcement for positive reinforcement training, some owners prefer to use this training method as their primary method of training. Using a clicker allows you to indicate to your dog the exact behavior that you're rewarding him for and is a great method to utilize when teaching new tricks.

- Shock Training

Shock training relies on the use of an electric collar to correct behaviors or to keep a dog within a certain area. This sort of training is not recommended for regular dog owners. Not only does it create pain and stress for a dog, it also does not correct the behavior; it only teaches the dog what behavior is bad and not what is good.

- Relationship-Based Training

As the name suggests, relationship-based training focuses on building the relationship between dog and owner by controlling the dog's environment and implementing communication to understand the root of the behaviors being corrected. This method uses a lot of training principles from other training methods, especially positive reinforcement, but the primary difference between this method and other methods is that this method of training focuses on being mutually beneficial for both dog and owner. This method of training may take longer than others but will foster a strong, long-lasting relationship between you and your Beagle.

Basic Commands

Basic commands are so easy to teach a dog, and they really can make your life easier and less stressful. I've tripped over a clingy Arthur a lot while working around the house, but when Arthur was finally old enough to start training, "stay" was the third command he learned (right behind "sit" and "lie down," which are his favorite commands to follow). For Beagles, you should begin training between three to six months. You'll know the right time for your dog if you just start out practicing "sit" around the three-month mark.

Each dog-training session usually lasts about 15 minutes, and it doesn't take a dog long at all to catch on to a new skill. Sit is one of the easiest skills to teach a dog, and I consider it the basis by which dogs learn every other command. The method by which I practice training Arthur always starts in the sit position, and it lets Arthur know we're about to start a training session.

Photo Courtesy of
Larissa Pyer

If you follow these methods (whether as a unit or separai should find that it's not much trouble to have a well-trained Beaௗ

The only tools you'll need to begin your Beagle's training are ੌ ੋong leash (which is really optional) and some treats.

Tie the leash securely around something sturdy so your Beagle can't roam far but can still be "away" from you when needed. This method can teach your Beagle sit, stay, lie down, and begin teaching her come.

For Arthur, I actually prefer to use two-word commands just because Arthur seems to respond better to "sit down" rather than just "sit," and "stay there/come here," rather than just "stay/come." Whatever phrase you use, stay consistent, and make sure everyone who will be around your dog regularly knows these commands.

Make sure the training area you've chosen is somewhere your dog can be comfortable. When I practiced with Arthur, we did so in the front yard, and I tied him to a post on the porch.

Teaching the Sit Down Command

The reason you really need treats to start training most dogs, especially Beagles, is that the easiest way to get a dog to sit is to lure her into the sitting position with a treat.

To guide your pup into the sitting position, hold the treat up and over your Beagle's nose, slowly lifting the treat away from her mouth and toward the back of her head. Your Beagle should sit down in order to get access to the treat, at which point you should reward her behavior with a treat and a kind word.

Practice this move several times, now combining it with the "sit" or "sit down" command. Try walking a few steps away, repeating the command, and rewarding your pup a few more times so she has a chance to understand the connection between her behavior and her getting a yummy treat.

Make sure your command comes before you move the treat above your dog's head. The treat is a reward for following a command, NOT a reason to complete the command in the first place. You also want to reward the behavior as soon as your dog displays it. Dogs can easily become confused about why you're giving them a treat. If you delay rewards as your Beagle begins moving on to a different behavior because she feels nothing is forthcoming from you, and then you mistakenly reward this new behavior, confusion sets in.

Teaching the Stay There Command

After your dog has consistently sat both with AND without a treat (still give a verbal reward or use a clicker if that is the method of training you choose), it's time to move on to "stay."

"Stay" is a bit tricky because people sometimes reward their pups too soon or start off the training with too much distance between them and their pup. The farther away you are from your Beagle, the less likely she is to listen to you. But as long as you get the distance and timing right, teaching "stay" should be painless.

You, of course, want to start off with the "sit" command. This leaves your pup in a comfortable and stationary position to stay in as well as gains her attention for your next command.

Follow up your Beagle's successful completion of the "sit" command with a "stay" command, taking a single step back and away from your Beagle to start. You can increase the distances slowly as your Beagle's ability to control herself improves. If you're training a particularly young

Photo Courtesy of Adrienne Rothenberg

Beagle, you may want to start off kneeling directly in front of your dog and just leaning back slightly. Puppies are clingy and are unlikely to give you space because they want to be close.

Reward your Beagle if you see that she's trying, even if she gets up a little early. She has a lot of energy and excitement not only because you're paying attention to her but also because she knows she's getting treats in the process.

Note that when you're teaching new skills and practicing with old ones, you want to reward your pup after she's performed the new behavior unless you feel you need to reinforce the previous skill.

Teaching the Lie Down Command

When you're teaching the "lie down" command, it's important that you yourself have an idea about what "lying down" is. In dog training, "down" is a position in which a dog has her belly to the ground and her elbows touching her belly.

Dogs may sometimes crouch instead of completely lying down, so make sure you're rewarding your Beagle when she's in the correct position. Dogs are very aware of their bodies and the positions they are in, and you don't want your Beagle to be reward for being in a "half sitting/half ready to run" position.

Start with your pup in the sit position. This position smoothly transitions your Beagle from sitting to lying. When you get her into the sit position, don't give her the treat, but do give her a verbal reward. Continue moving the treat down from your dog's nose to the floor between her legs until your dog's nose touches the floor and she achieves the down position.

If your Beagle manages to keep standing up and walking toward the food instead of lying down, you have the food too far away from her. Bring it closer so the treat is more tempting for her and it is easier for you to guide her into the down position.

After consistently getting her into the position, begin using her name when telling her to lie down.

Usually, when I'm telling Arthur to lie down, it's inside of his kennel, and he does so eagerly because I'm using an inviting voice and inviting him to a place he enjoys being.

Teaching the Come Here Command

Remember that this command should always end in something positive for your dog. Imagine if every time you came when someone called, you were punished or put inside your kennel while all of your family left the house. Dogs are smart, and your dog can quickly associate certain commands with negative experiences. Beagles are independent enough to ignore commands for many reasons. Along the same lines, avoid using your dog's name when telling her to come, unless you have multiple pets. In that case, the names are used to distinguish who the command is for.

Let your dog roam away from you while on the leash, and when he's far enough away, lightly tug on the leash and say, "Come here." Your dog should understand, and you should reward his understanding and completion of the desired action with a treat and a verbal reward so he understands what action you are rewarding. While Beagles do like to roam, they can also be clingy, so you may have to throw some treats away from you if your Beagle is the kind of dog to stick to you like glue.

Practice this move inside and outside, leashed and unleashed. When your Beagle comes, firmly but gently grip her collar and give her praise so she knows that coming when called is a good thing.

Teaching the Get Down/Off Command

Whether it's down from the couch or down from leaning or jumping on you, your dog really needs to learn this command. From scratching up your couch to scratching up your leg, your dog will jump and lean and scratch in the process, so this command is important to learn to minimize destruction/injury.

With this command, I prefer "get off" because dogs may get confused if they're already learning to lie down. You see how avoiding single-word commands can improve learning?

You need a lot of patience when teaching this command because this behavior is so natural for a dog. Beagles, especially, want to stand and lean on everything to get a better whiff of something, even if that something is a human leg. But young children can easily be knocked over by a hungry Beagle searching for snacks, so for safety, you don't want your Beagle leaning willy-nilly.

To teach the "get off" command, wait until your dog jumps or leans on someone or a piece or furniture she isn't allowed on. With a treat in hand, let your dog sniff the treat, then guide her nose down to the floor while giving the "get off" command. Give her the treat only when she's completely on the ground.

This behavior takes a while to reinforce, but consistency is key. Your dog can't be allowed on the furniture sometimes and not others.

Teaching the Leave/Drop it Command

Teaching the "leave it" command is so important both to prevent your dog from running off with other people's belongings as well as to prevent her from consuming something harmful.

Now, it's good to know what sort of things might interest your dog, to practice leaving your pup with something.

Dogs will try to discover or retrieve things on a walk, in someone's room, from a table, behind a door, and just generally any place they

*Photo Courtesy of
Samantha Marinovic*

HELPFUL TIP
Be Careful
with Treats

According to pets.webmd.com, your dog should receive only 10 percent of his calories from treats. Rawhide, produced and manufactured in the USA, should provide pleasure for your dog. It will soften as he licks it, unlike newer options on the market. Be cautious with hard treats such as antlers and bones. Dogs will enthusiastically bite down on these hard treats, often breaking teeth. Ask for advice from your veterinarian about specific treats that will be beneficial for your pet.

smell something interesting. As such, you want to practice this command in various situations.

Start off with two treats, one in the palm of each of your hands. Close your fingers around the treats, and let your Beagle sniff one of your hands. She will smell the treat and try her hardest to get to it, but you should tell your pup to "leave it," then reward her the moment she looks away. Important: feed your pup the treat from the OTHER hand.

After your Beagle has consistently left the treat alone, try different methods. Show your dog the treat, say "leave it," but close your hand if she attempts to take it from you. Repeat this process until she eventually leaves the treat alone and decides to ignore it. Remember not to give your Beagle the treat you've been keeping from her.

This training method can be done almost anywhere, and you don't even need to have this treat in your hand. Off the leash, you can just leave the treat on the floor and cover it with a bowl, your hand, your foot, a blanket, or really anything that still allows the smell of the treat to reach your dog's nose. On the leash, you can try these same items or just keep the leash taut enough to keep your dog from the treat. Don't forget to repeat the command until your dog performs the desired behavior, and again, give her a different treat from the one you want her to leave.

As for getting something out of your Beagle's mouth, surprise! Treats are, again, necessary to teach this skill. Practice with your pup by giving her some of her things to chew on. Once she has the object in her mouth, place the treat next to her nose and give the "drop it" command. Praise your pup when she drops what she's holding, and give her the treat as you take the item from the floor.

Practice this move throughout the day with your dog. Sessions that last too long may end with your Beagle refusing to pick up anything else. Just give her a break, and wait for her to pick something else to practice with.

As your dog gets better at this command, practice with harder-to-release items like their favorite toys or a slow-eating treat.

Teaching the Walk/Heel Command

First, make sure you have treats on hand, and choose a side of your body you want your dog to walk on (left is traditional in competitions).

Call your dog's name, then point to the side you've chosen. When she comes to your side, praise and reward her. Repeat this action until she's consistently completing it, then stop pointing to your side. Reward your dog each time she comes up beside you.

To practice this skill more, walk, run, and zigzag to try throwing your dog off. She'll get better at this command AND will enjoy running around and chasing you.

Advanced Commands

If your dog easily masters basic commands, there are definitely more commands you can teach him. In fact, dogs are able to learn over 165 words, and commands don't have to be verbal. Dogs also understand hand commands, so there are endless skills you can teach your dog.

Advanced commands can strengthen your dog's intelligence and prepare him for dog sports and agility shows.

Here are some popular advanced skills to teach your Beagle:

- Leap
- Spin
- Shake
- Bow
- Speak

CHAPTER 12
Dealing With Unwanted Behaviors

"When teething sometimes puppies will become nippy and bite. Those little teeth hurt! Unfortunately at first many new owners allow this because it seems harmless. Do not ever play rough or in any manner that encourages biting. If you do have this issue, show that displeasure to your puppy through stopping"

Jennifer Eaton Lopez
Little Beagles

Photo Courtesy of Casey Murdough

Photo Courtesy of
Dana Mong

What is Bad Behavior in Dogs?

There isn't one true definition of bad behavior in dogs because different owners teach their dogs different behaviors that are acceptable to display. Some pet parents don't mind if their animals are on the furniture while others may want to emphasize the "get down" command in their training. Regardless of what you think bad behavior is in your dog, understanding the root of the behavior your dog is displaying can help you influence the direction of that behavior more easily than punishment, which doesn't work for dogs when they don't understand the reason for being punished.

Bad behavior in dogs can stem from lack of training, lack of exercise, lack of mental stimulation, changes in routine, poor socialization, fear, health problems, and more. Bad behavior is rarely caused by your dog wanting to act out. In most cases, your dog just doesn't know the proper actions to take either because he hasn't been trained or he hasn't been well-trained.

Some common behavioral problems include biting, aggression, chasing, begging, digging, and barking.

To prevent these problems and eliminate them, figure out where these behaviors stem from. After you've pinpointed the problem, then you can work on it.

Preventing and Correcting Common Bad Behaviors

Aggression is the most common bad behavior seen in dogs because it's what wild dogs use to defend themselves, so aggression can be caused by fear, protective behavior, or a medical problem among other things. Aggression displays itself by the dog becoming still, growling, baring its teeth, snarling, and other behaviors that indicate a dog is preparing to attack. Aggression can't be prevented immediately, but some things you can do to reduce aggression involve keeping your dog leashed, so he doesn't have the opportunity to be aggressive with other dogs, and desensitizing your dog to the fear triggering the aggression. To truly correct this behavior, you have to discover the source of the aggression.

Chasing can be a hazard to both your dog and other animals. Your dog could run into the street attempting to chase a car, or your dog could be chasing a cat and injure or kill it. To prevent chasing, you must train your dog to listen to the basic commands. It is your responsibility to ensure that your dog does not harm other animals. Cat chasing may be fun to your dog, but your neighbors will NOT appreciate if you haven't trained your Beagle (that was used for hunting small game!) to not run off and chase anything that moves. Keeping your dog leashed or otherwise contained will prevent most occurrences of chasing. To correct chasing, try to redirect your dog's attention if you catch him barking/being interested in something chaseable. Offer, instead, to play with your dog with some of his toys.

Chewing is natural for dogs! To prevent chewing, make sure your dog has plenty to chew on such as toys and hard treats and be sure to teach your dog what he is and isn't allowed to chew on. To correct this behavior, redirect the chewing to an appropriate item. Exchange a stolen sock for a stuffed toy.

Barking can be caused by many things (which I outline in the "Being a Puppy Parent" chapter of this book), so to prevent this behavior, identify the cause to treat the problem. If your dog is barking for attention, firmly give him the quiet command and make him sit. Teach your Beagle a new behavior to replace the barking behavior. For instance, if he barks whenever someone comes to the door, train him to instead go and pick up a toy to present to your guest. He can't bark if his mouth is full.

Biting, like chewing, is natural for dogs and how they interact with the world, but your dog needs to learn that it isn't okay to bite humans. You may not mind if your puppy bites your hand, especially if he's gentle or his bites don't hurt yet. As he gets older, of course, his bites will get stronger. To prevent biting, don't allow your puppy to bite your hands.

*Photo Courtesy of
Deborah Smith*

HELPFUL TIP
When to Call
a Professional

If your dog is exhibiting behaviors such as whining, howling, barking, or being destructive, it may be time to call in a professional to assist with training. Some dogs suffer from separation anxiety that leads them to these unwanted behaviors. Dogs will whine and bark from boredom. If you feel you have exercised your dog well, trained him, and offered many opportunities for socialization, and this conduct continues, call in an expert. You want your dog to be content, and once that happens, you will also be happy with the behavior changes.

Provide him with plenty of things to chew on other than you. To correct this behavior, loudly imitate a dog's yelp and walk away from your dog. He will soon learn that this behavior is unwanted.

Jumping or pawing happens usually because your dog is excited about something or really wants your attention. This behavior usually starts when the dog is a small puppy and the behavior isn't too bothersome, but as dogs get older, the behavior gets more bothersome. Prevent this behavior early by teaching and practicing the "get down" command. To correct this behavior, turn away from your dog and ignore him. Pushing him away is giving him attention, which is what he wants, but walking away does not reward his behavior. When your dog comes to you for attention again, make him sit first, then reward him for this desired behavior.

Dogs mount other dogs to show dominance. It's not always aggressive or sexually motivated. A dog may attempt to mount anyone, including small children if the dog sees them as below them in the pack. Calmly push your dog away and walk away without saying anything if your dog attempts to mount you or an adult. If a child is the target, firmly give the "get off" command. Your dog should quickly learn that this behavior is inappropriate and unwanted.

Many dogs eat feces if given the chance, their own, or that of any animal they can find (usually cats). This behavior is unhealthy for many reasons (they lick your face with that mouth!), but the primary concern is the transference of diseases and worms that may be present within another animal's feces. To prevent this behavior, make sure your dog doesn't have access to another animal's poop. He's far less likely to eat his own poop, but if he does have a habit of eating his own poop, pick it up before he has a chance to eat it. If you catch your dog in the act of eating poop, try scaring your dog with a loud noise while avoiding letting your dog know the noise came from you (otherwise, he'll just hide the behavior from you better).

Marking can easily be prevented by getting your dog spayed or neutered when they reach six months of age. Marking can be caused by territorial feelings, leftover smell from a previous marking, or leftover smell from another animal's marking. The longer a dog goes without being fixed, the harder it will be to correct this behavior later on. If your dog is already older and has already been marking for a while, spaying or neutering won't help. In that case, you must, instead, house-train the adult dog.

Remember, when you're correcting your Beagle's behavior, you don't want to yell, scream, or physical punish your dog. Your dog considers himself a part of your family, and if you've added a Beagle to your family, then you should already be prepared to treat your Beagle like a member of your family.

You want to focus on reinforcing the behaviors you want your Beagle to display. Reinforcing good behaviors will naturally reduce the occurrences of bad behavior, so you will have fewer reasons to discipline your Beagle.

*Photo Courtesy of
Beth Forbey*

Catching your dog in the middle of the behavior you want to discourage will also reduce these occurrences. Your dog truly won't understand why he is in trouble if you don't discipline him while in the act or directly after the act. Just keep your eyes open for sneaky or naughty behavior.

And generally, just try to redirect your dog's attention. Dogs aren't good at staying focused when they have something more interesting being offered to them. This can be treats, toys, playtime, praise, the offer of a walk, or really anything your dog enjoys. And your dog will soon learn that good behavior is rewarded well with the things he loves

If you know from the start that you don't have time to properly train your dog and correct his behaviors, hire a professional from the beginning. Doing so will save you a lot of strife and possibly, money and time.

If you have been training your dog yourself, the best time to call a professional is when you come upon a behavior your dog simply won't learn or unlearn. Professionals, obviously, have more experience correcting dogs of many different breeds, and chances are, they will be able to help you easily. You may benefit from watching a professional train your dog to the point that you no longer need to hire someone to help train your dog.

Beagle-Specific Bad Habits

"The number one complaint is unwanted barking. This is usually a sign that they are bored and need more interaction with the family."

Dennis Dollar
Barrister Beagles

Beagles are smart and can be very naughty. Watch out for these habits of Beagles:

1. Beagles will steal food from plates, counters, tables, food dishes, trash cans, directly from hands, or directly from mouths. Beagles are hungry puppies; they will willingly disobey if they think they can sneak even a bite of food.

2. Beagles can also be destructive when not given enough exercise or stimulation. Chewing is number one on the list for destructive Beagle behavior, and sometimes even when a Beagle has plenty of his own toys to chew, he will retrieve and chew on anything he can find.

3. Beagles can be slow to housebreak. Many "accidents" will be hidden around your house. Leash training inside will help train both you and your pup on his house-training schedule.

4. Beagles can have independent attitudes ... meaning they will ignore your commands if they find something better to interest them. Their stubbornness can make them wander off, even if you are giving the much-practiced "come here" command.

CHAPTER 13
Traveling With Beagles

"Beagles love to travel. The compact size and natural curiosity makes them perfect travel companions."

Jennifer Eaton Lopez
Little Beagles

Photo Courtesy of Colby Diamond

Traveling with your Beagle in a car should be relatively easy since Beagles are typically intelligent, social, and calm dogs. They can be full of energy, though, so you want to plan for plenty of potty/walk breaks.

The most important part of your trip is the planning because you can't just pack your dog into the car and take off. Dogs have needs just as we do, and while some of us can drive 10 hours at a time with no problem, your Beagle may have a problem being in a car for that long, especially if you haven't properly prepared to keep her comfortable.

Just like humans need to wear seatbelts for safety, dogs should be secured inside of a car for safe travel for the safety of everyone in the car and on the road. Letting your dog roam free in your car can lead to the injury or even death of your beloved Beagle or anyone else in the car. Dogs can also be a huge distraction on the road, which can cause you to harm other drivers, so make sure when you travel with your dog that he is inside of a dog carrier or secured with another type of car restraint.

When searching for a travel carrier, it's important to do your research about the safety of the carrier. Not every carrier is created equally, and even if the carrier claims to be designed for car travel, you want to make sure the carrier will truly keep your dog secure during a long trip when anything could happen.

Choosing a Car Restraint

Size is an important consideration when choosing a travel carrier as a carrier that is too big may allow your dog to be injured because there's too much room to move around. A car carrier shouldn't be more than six inches longer than your dog's body. For a Beagle, the appropriate carrier size will likely be between 30 and 36 inches, depending on your pet's size and weight.

Photo Courtesy of
Alicia Blain

There are a variety of car-restraint types to choose from including closed crates and kennels, an open car seat, a backseat barrier, or even a simple car harness.

I, personally, recommend a kennel or crate since they are typically sturdier, easier to keep in place, and, depending on their size, can hold multiple pets. The placement of the crate is important—cars have "crumple areas" at the front and back that help reduce impact on the middle of the car, so putting your dog's crate in the trunk is likely a bad idea. The front seat is also a bad idea because airbags are meant to keep humans alive, not dogs.

A dog car seat is usually plush like a pet bed and open to the car. These seats are meant to be strapped to seatbelts and often have restraints to attach to your dog's harness. A car seat is typically used for smaller dogs so they can see higher, but you should still be cautious with this option as it may not provide as much safety to your Beagle as other car- restraint options.

A backseat barrier is a good option if you prefer to let your dog roam the backseat. From sturdy metal to mesh cloth, these barriers can be as complicated as covering your entire backseat or as simple as a barrier preventing your dog from entering the front seat. The danger that comes with a backseat barrier is that your dog is loose and may be thrown around the back in an accident.

A car harness is probably the simplest option. Car harnesses are designed to protect your dog from the impact of a crash and to keep your dog from roaming the car too much, so don't use just any harness if you choose this option for travel. Make sure the harness has wide straps to keep your dog comfortable and to reduce injury during a crash.

*Photo Courtesy of
Matt Lovelace*

Preparing Your Dog for Car Rides

Safety is only the first aspect of traveling to consider with your dog. Though your pet may be safe for the drive to whatever destination you're headed toward, he may not enjoy the ride as much as you'd hope.

Although some dogs love a good car ride, even a long one, other dogs absolutely hate the idea of setting foot inside of a car for one reason or another. Maybe your dog suffers from car-related anxiety or gets carsick on long rides. Either way, if you must take your furry friend with you on a trip, you must first prepare him for the ride.

A big reason a dog may be anxious about cars is that his only experience with car rides is going to the vet or groomer, and most dogs detest the vet and groomer. If your dog seems to dislike car rides, give him a fresh experience by associating car rides with more pleasant destinations. Go to the park, take a trip to the pet store, or visit a good friend! Doggy playdates are important anyway, so there are plenty of opportunities to diversify your dog's view of the car.

This tactic of preparing your dog for a trip should be ongoing throughout the dog's life; after all, you never know when you may have to take a trip across the country, to begin with. There may be an unplanned vacation or a far-off emergency to tend to. Make sure your dog is ready for car trips ahead of time to make whatever the situation is far less stressful for both you and your dog.

The goal here is to make car rides neutral and calm. You don't want your dog overly excited while in the car, and you don't want him to be afraid or anxious either.

If your dog already has a negative association with your car, use the same tactics for introducing your Beagle to his crate to convince him to get inside of your car. Let your dog adjust slowly to the car over a few days or weeks, then start going on short car rides (maybe to the dog park?). Keep up this practice, and your dog should be ready for longer trips in time.

If your dog does not become acclimated to car rides, you may need to consult your veterinarian about medication to either ease your dog's anxiety or to sedate your dog for the trip.

Make sure to feed your dog well before you leave for your trip, with sufficient time for a long walk so he may relieve himself and become tired out.

Keeping Your Dog on a Routine

Even though a car ride may be a break from your dog's routine, you should attempt to keep your dog on his usual routine. That means planning stops around your dog's regular potty schedule or eating times.

If you have enough time to plan before your trip, see which cities you will be passing through at certain times. Plan to stop at a dog-friendly location in that city such as a dog park, a beach, or just an area good for walking your dog around.

A problem many owners find is that their dog refuses to use the bathroom somewhere unfamiliar, so before your trip, it's a good idea to train your dog to use the bathroom on command or to familiarize your dog with using the bathroom away from home and other familiar areas.

Flying With Your Dog

If you're flying instead of driving, your trip will likely be much shorter, but you will also have less control over the safety and comfort of your beloved pet. Doing your research before choosing an airline can save you a lot of grief. Some airlines have bad reputations regarding traveling with pets, so choose carefully and be aware that most airlines require advanced reservations for pet travel and also have differing policies on pet travel.

After you've chosen an appropriate airline, you must then prepare your dog for flying. Flying is likely to be far more stressful to your dog than a car ride, especially since you may not be allowed to be near your dog on the trip. Different airlines have different policies, though, so aim for an airline that allows you to have your pet in the cabin with you.

Typically, a pet-friendly airline will, for a fee, allow small dogs inside of a carrier to ride inside of the cabin with their owners, provided the dog stays within the carrier for the whole flight. As such, and as with all dog carriers, your carrier should have enough room for your dog to comfortably stand up and turn around in. Flights can be long, and your pup is likely unused to the experience, so make sure you acclimate your dog to being inside of a carrier for long periods of time if this is the option you go with.

Unfortunately, most Beagles won't qualify for cabin travel because of common airline weight and size limits. Airlines require that the carrier and dog, together, weigh no more than about 20 pounds, and the carrier must fit underneath the seat in front of you. Since you want your Beagle to be comfortable, do not force an oversized dog into a small carrier just to get them into the cabin with you. Most airlines have a policy about a dog's comfort inside of the carrier, regardless, but it's important to state that your dog deserves comfort.

Being inside of the cargo hold can be traumatic for pets, so you might consider leaving your Beagle at home if you are unable to carry him in the cabin with you. The flight itself, regardless of where your dog is on the plane, is likely to stress your dog out, so consider calming pheromone collars or sprays, sedatives, or anti-anxiety/nausea medication prescribed by a veterinarian.

*Photo Courtesy of
Janet Lam*

Hotel Stays With Your Dog

If you're going on an especially long drive, you'll likely have to spend the night in a hotel. It's not a good idea to stay in just any hotel, especially if you haven't checked that establishment's pet policy. Pet-friendly airlines and hotels exist and are plentiful, but finding them may require research beforehand, and most require that you make a reservation before you arrive for your stay.

HELPFUL TIP

Bon Voyage!

So you are going on a vacation or away for work. What should you do with your pet while you're gone? Kennels may offer cage-free boarding that can assist with socialization. Check with friends and family members to see if there are reputable kennels near you. Although this option may be ideal for younger dogs, some older dogs may become anxious in this environment. Pet sitters are another option available to pet owners who travel. Do your homework, however, before opening your home to a stranger. Definitely ask for references from a potential dog sitter. Checking with your veterinarian is also a wise option. Better safe than sorry when it comes to the care of your loving companion.

Three of the most common pet-friendly hotel chains include La Quinta, Motel 6, and Best Western, but websites such as orbitz.com allow you to search for hotels that accept furry companions and even offer "pet-menities" that rival the amenities offered for humans. It's definitely worth the research to find a hotel that fits your needs and which can offer your pet a new way to be spoiled.

I suggest requesting a room on the ground floor since you'll need to make several trips outside for potty breaks. Being on the ground floor will also make carting your belongings in and out less of a hassle. You probably don't want to unload all of your baggage for each trip, so make sure your dogs have easy-to-carry overnight luggage for hotel rooms.

Once you're actually inside of your hotel room, make sure your dog has a comfortable place to rest. A hotel room will be new and smell strange to your dog, so plan ahead with packing to make sure your dog feels comforted by familiar items such as his favorite blanket, toys, or dog bed.

Playing with your dog inside the room will make him comfortable because he'll see that you are comfortable and unworried.

Again, keep your pup on a routine! Hotels do charge deposits for pets in case of property damage, so to ensure you get your deposit back, make sure you're taking your dog out to do his business regularly.

Whenever you need to go in and out of your hotel room, you may consider leaving your pup in the bathroom if he is likely to run outside the first chance he gets. You don't want your Beagle to be lost in a strange city.

I don't recommend leaving your Beagle alone in the room if you can avoid it. He's likely to already be frightened at his new surroundings, and if you leave him alone (especially uncrated!), he may become destructive and loud, resulting in fees for you and complaints from the other visitors. If you do need to leave your dog alone, make sure you leave the lights and TV on.

If you're at your vacation destination and staying in a hotel, consider local doggy daycare or other dog services if one of your planned activities isn't dog-friendly.

Be aware that some hotels have policies against leaving pets unattended in rooms for some periods of time or at all. Part of the reason for this policy is that hotels often reimburse customers for disturbances such as excessive dog barking or howling. Policies such as this one also encourage dog owners to be more respectful of other hotel guests.

Photo Courtesy of
Scott Pendlebury

Kenneling vs. Dog Sitters

Sometimes, taking your dog on a trip with you just isn't an option. Maybe your dog doesn't do well on the road, or maybe he's too big to travel in the cabin of a plane with you and you'd rather not put him through the stress of traveling with the cargo.

Regardless of why your Beagle can't join you on your travels, there are certainly options for leaving your Beagle while you travel.

The simplest option is to ask a friend, neighbor, or family member to dog sit for you. Someone your Beagle knows is likely to have an easier job of caring for your pet and will make your Beagle feel more comfortable.

If you don't know someone who is able to dog sit, there are many companies and individuals who offer dog-sitting services or dog drop-in services. A dog sitter will either stay in your home to care for your dog or care for your dog within their own home. A drop-in service will come to your home to take care of your dog once or twice a day.

Pet sitting or a drop-in service is a good option if you've got multiple pets. Other furry companions will keep your Beagle from loneliness while you're gone, and a drop-in service can just ensure that all your pets are fed and let out regularly.

Kenneling is another option for your pet. Kenneling or boarding services are like hotels for dogs. Many of these kenneling services offer amenities for dogs during their stay as well.

Which option you choose depends on you and your dog. Some dogs are fine with being alone for most of the day, but keep in mind the length of your trip. A young dog will NOT be fine alone for long at all. A pet sitter is probably best for a younger dog.

Kenneling, depending on the service you go with, can offer your dog plenty of socialization with other dogs and other humans. Kenneling can vary in pricing depending on the amenities, but this option has been the most popular for years, and many pet owners just prefer kenneling over pet sitting. Kenneling is probably the best option if your home area may experience bad weather around the time of your trip.

I personally recommend hiring a pet sitter (someone you know, if possible). Your dog will be much more comfortable being in familiar surroundings or with a familiar person. A kennel is also likely to be housing other anxious dogs, which can make your dog more anxious and stressed in the process.

Regardless of the service you choose, make sure you research the person or company you're leaving your furry family member with. If your Beagle has special needs or medications he needs to take, make sure whoever you leave your Beagle with has all the information and tools necessary to take care of your pup.

Tips and Tricks for Traveling

1. Before you take a long trip, practice long drives with your dog to see how he does. You may realize that a long car ride is not for your Beagle after all.

2. Make sure your dog has clothes for your destination! If you're going somewhere cold, splurge on winter clothes and shoes to keep your tiny friend warm.

3. Pack a pet first-aid kit! You never know what will happen. Not only should you have a first-aid kit with you; you should also learn and practice some life-saving medical training.

4. Visit your vet before your trip, and get your dog cleared for travel. You can also discuss sedatives or anxiety medicine while there.

5. Plan pet-friendly activities for during your trip as well as at your destination.

6. Line your dog's carrier with a puppy pad. Accidents happen!

7. Make sure you're allowed to take your Beagle to your destination if you're traveling outside of the country.

8. Avoid leaving your Beagle alone in your car, even with the windows cracked. Someone could steal him, or he could overheat or freeze.

9. Don't feed your Beagle while the car is moving! Use one of your scheduled breaks as a feeding break.

10. Consider getting your dog chipped before your trip.

Other Supplies to Pack
- Collapsible food and water bowls
- Food and water
- Calming pet music (YouTube has several videos)
- Updated pet identification tags
- Waste bags

CHAPTER 14
Nutrition

"Beagles are known for cast iron stomachs, and can be very heavy eaters so self-feeders are usually not suggested. Just about any average to good quality feed is acceptable; however weigh control is very important so a weight maintenance formula is ideal as they get older."

Gregg Moore
Moore Beagles

Importance of Good Diet

You can help ensure that your Beagle lives a long and healthy life by providing her with a well-balanced diet.

A well-balanced diet is vital for your dog, especially since Beagles are prone to overeating and obesity. Overweight Beagles are prone to many more health problems than Beagles who are a healthy weight. Obesity in animals is just as serious as it is in humans, so be strict with your Beagle and watch his intake of calories.

The most important part of any living creature's diet is, of course, water, so make sure your Beagle has access to clean water.

I don't give my Beagle, Arthur, unlimited access to water. He will drink an entire bowl if given the chance, and when he was still being house-trained, this meant that he would pee in the house several times an hour. As such, I placed his water bowl outside in the backyard and now allow him to drink from it freely either when he's outside playing or during scheduled potty breaks. Arthur is discouraged from drinking water until after he has gone potty, but do not keep your dog from drinking water altogether!

A balanced diet for a dog includes proteins, fats, carbs, minerals, and vitamins. Most commercial pet foods provide the mix of nutrients dogs need, but do your research and read the label to ensure your dog is getting the proper nutrients.

Proper nutrients helps maintain your dog's muscles, skin, coat, joints, digestion, and more. Without the necessary nutrients, your dog

*Photo Courtesy of
Jamie Lapusnik*

wouldn't be able to build or repair muscles, maintain healthy teeth and bones, or perform her normal daily activities.

The exact food requirements for your dog will vary based on her activity level, age, stress level, and medical history. Outdoor pets are more likely to need a protein-heavy dog food. Puppies require more calories than adult dogs because they are still growing.

Commercial dog foods are often labeled for different needs, so choosing a commercial food that's right for your dog is all about looking around, getting recommendations, and seeing for yourself what works best for your Beagle.

Good Foods for Beagles

The average Beagle weighs 22 pounds and requires between 533-910 calories, depending on how active she is. Beagles typically burn a lot of calories, though, so a dog food high in protein or designed for high-energy breeds is the way to go.

From eye diseases to irritable bowel syndrome to bladder cancer, Beagles are prone to several health problems that pet food can help counter.

Some of the best dog foods for Beagles will provide nutrients specifically for the breed and its common health problems. Look for ingredients such as lutein, zinc, and selenium for eye care; glucosamine and chondroitin for hip dysplasia; low-carb, high-protein foods for bladder cancer and obesity; and high-fiber, grain-free foods for irritable bowel syndrome.

In general, look for pet foods with whole protein as the first ingredient(s), without unidentified animal products, and without artificial flavors or additives. It's not 100 percent necessary to address every disease-fighting nutrient when choosing a dog food since dog foods, in general, are designed to keep dogs healthy and provide the general nutrients they need.

Commercial Food Options

With a variety of commercial pet foods on the market, it can be overwhelming to choose one that's right for your Beagle. There are a few trusted brands to keep in mind, though, that you can rarely go wrong with.

Benefits

Royal Canin Beagle Adult Dry Dog Food offers a tailor-made kibble that helps your Beagle maintain an ideal weight, controls her food intake, and supports her bone and join health.

- Designed specifically for adult Beagles
- Supports healthy bones and joints
- Kibble shape encourages slower eating for healthier ingestion
- Contains appropriate calorie content to help maintain an ideal weight

Blue Buffalo Life Protection Formula Adult Chicken & Brown Rice Recipe Dry Dog Food is another great option since it boasts real meat, whole grains, fruits, vegetables, and other added nutrients to support your dog's life-long wellbeing.

- Supports strong bones and teeth
- Includes glucosamine for joint health and mobility support
- Includes a mix of nutrients that support your dog's immune system
- Does not include wheat, corn, soy, or chicken by-product meals.

Blue Buffalo Wilderness High Protein Grain-Free, Natural Wet Dog Food is a great choice for picky eaters with its natural mixes of grilled meats.

- Variety of flavors such as beef, chicken, salmon, turkey, duck, and more
- Inspired by a wolf's diet
- Contains no meat by-product meals, wheat, corn, soy, or artificial preservatives

Orijen Regional Red justifies its high price point by providing kibble specifically formulated to mimic a dog's natural diet.

- Full of natural and fresh animal protein such as boar, lamb, and beef
- Ingredients are farmed, caught, and grown in the USA
- Doesn't contain preservatives
- Free of allergy-causing grains

Taste of The Wild Grain-Free High- Protein Dry Dog Food provides a limited-ingredient diet full of real meat, fish, and fowl, flavored specifically for your pet's taste buds.

- Contains real roasted meat
- Free of allergy-causing grains
- Contains a mix of fruits and vegetables high in antioxidants
- Recipe mimics the diet of your dog's ancestors

Homemade Foods, Recipes

Homemade dog food and pet treats can be a great alternative to commercial dog foods as long as you are providing your dog with the nutritional diet she needs to be strong and healthy. You may want to make homemade dog food to keep your dog safe from harmful substances in some commercial foods, to save money, or just to have the peace of mind of knowing exactly what goes into your pet's body.

Making your dog meals from scratch is the same as making your own meals from scratch and will be easier since you don't have to worry about seasoning at all. While the actual process of making your dog's food at home is simple, though, finding recipes that provide all the nutrients your dog needs is a bit trickier. Choosing a recipe created by a certified animal or pet nutritionist can help in this case.

Your dog needs protein, calcium, essential fatty acids, carbohydrates, fiber, vitamins, minerals, and antioxidants, but since these nutrients are also vital for humans, you shouldn't have any trouble actually finding appropriate ingredients to include in your dog's food.

Some Common Ingredients That Can Help Address Your Dog's Dietary Needs:

Protein	Chicken, beef, turkey, duck, lamb, venison, fish, beans, eggs, meat meal, cheese
Carbohydrates	White or brown rice, potatoes, sweet potatoes, oatmeal, barley
Calcium	Yogurt, cheese, broccoli, spinach, beans, tuna, salmon, bone meal, ground eggshells
Essential fatty acids	Salmon, mackerel, halibut, herring, flaxseed oil, coconut oil, canola oil, walnut oil, soy
Fiber	Carrots, milled flaxseed, kale, pumpkins, apples, broccoli, green beans, bran, wheatgerm, beans
Antioxidants	Apples, beans, cabbage, pecans, strawberries, broccoli
Vitamins	Vitamin A (carrots, eggs, leafy greens)
	Vitamin B (cauliflower, fish, wheatgerm, cheese, eggs, nuts, beans, broccoli)
	Vitamin C (berries, oranges, tangerines, clementines, tomatoes, leafy greens)
	Vitamin D (fish, cheese, yogurt, eggs)
	Vitamin E (spinach, corn, nuts, wheatgerm)
	Vitamin K (cabbage, leafy greens, cauliflower)
Minerals	Iron (chicken, turkey, kale, spinach)
	Selenium (tuna, halibut, beef)
	Zinc (chicken, turkey, spinach)
	Copper (kale, spinach, flaxseed)
	Manganese (chicken, salmon, eggs, spinach)

Recipes for how to make your dog's food can either be self-created with the help of a nutritionist or found online by a trusted source. When using a recipe, it's important to know exactly what each ingredient is providing to your pup so that you can substitute that ingredient with one that will provide the same nutrients and number of calories. If you're planning to make your dog's food at home, you probably want to buy certain ingredients in bulk so you'll always have what the recipe calls for on hand.

Also, consider adding supplements to your homemade dog food. Commercial foods include many added supplements and nutrients that benefit your dog, but you can add some yourself, especially since not every recipe will provide all the nutrients your dog needs. Speak with your veterinarian or a pet nutritionist about which supplements to give your dog.

It's also a good idea to take your Beagle to the vet before you start an at-home meal plan for her so you can check her weight and health a few weeks after being on the homemade dog food diet.

Be cautious about what, exactly, you give your Beagle. People food can be harmful to your Beagle's health for many reasons. For one, human food often doesn't provide dogs with the balance of nutrition their bodies require. Additionally, a lot of human food includes extra salt or sugars that can contribute to weight problems or other medical problems. Limit the use of butter, cooking oils, corn, and dairy when cooking for your dog.

Raw meat may seem like an obviously good choice for your dog, but raw meat can contain bacteria that makes your dog sick, and meat, in general, may have bones that may harm your dog's teeth, the inside of her mouth, her throat, or her stomach.

People food can also be toxic. Onions, garlic, grapes, some citrus fruits, coffee, and chocolate are examples of harmful human foods. See Chapter 3 for a list of foods you can give your Beagle and foods you should avoid altogether.

Weight Management

Obesity in canines is one of the highest health concerns for dogs today. Obesity is defined as an excess of body fat which can come from overfeeding, underexercising, or some medical condition that can cause a dog to retain weight. Even just moderate obesity can reduce the lifespan of a dog and lead to join paint, digestive problems, and labored breathing.

HELPFUL TIP
Nutrition

Your Beagle is a sturdy dog; however, he needs quality food to maintain health and wellness. Consulting your vet or breeder regarding which nutritious food to offer your dog is the pathway to lifelong wellness. Whether you use purchased dog food or prepare your own homemade pet food, consult professionals to ensure he is getting the nutrition he needs. Care should be taken to offer age-appropriate food at the various stages of your dog's life. Puppy, adult, senior, and weight-control foods are widely available. Your Beagle may tend to gain weight if given too many treats and not enough exercise, so be mindful of the appropriate amount of food he needs daily.

Obesity in dogs can cause cardiac disease, diabetes, hypertension, ligament rupture, osteoarthritis, respiratory disorders, and various forms of cancer. Dogs who have been fixed, are middle-aged, or lead a sedentary indoor lifestyle are more at risk for obesity. A dog may gain weight if he is ill or recovering from an injury as he is less likely to be active at such a time. To pinpoint the exact cause of your dog's weight gain, speak with your veterinarian about possible causes.

Beagles love to eat, and if you want to help ensure your Beagle lives a long and happy life, it's vital that you manage your Beagle's diet as seriously as you manage your own, and even more so. Your sleek and muscled Beagle can easily become a sickly, obese Beagle without the proper care, and weight gain is more likely as your Beagle ages. You should begin lifelong healthy eating and exercise habits with your Beagle the moment she comes home.

There are things you can do to actively prevent your Beagle from becoming overweight. First off, you have control over what your Beagle eats. Follow the instructions on her food label for how much to feed her, and don't go over the recommended amount. Additionally, limit the number of snacks you feed your Beagle throughout the day as those can easily add up in calories. Consider using a portion of your Beagle's regular meal as treats for the day.

Beagles can sometimes have access to food you don't give them if you're not careful. If you have other animals in the house, your Beagle is likely to go for their food the moment you look away. If there are other dogs, free eating is a bad idea for all your dogs because your Beagle will just have everyone's portions. If you have cats, consider placing their food bowls where only they can reach them.

Let everyone in your household know to watch their food around your Beagle. A Beagle may try to steal food right off your plate if you're not careful, and Beagles aren't picky either. Spilled food or food from the trash is fair game. In addition to keeping your Beagle away from food, keep your dog on a consistent exercise routine, and she will be more likely to stay fit and trim.

Your veterinarian can tell you if your Beagle is overweight during one of her checkups, but you can tell yourself by looking at your Beagle from the top and the side. Your Beagle's waist should be defined, and you should see where her abdomen tucks into her rib cage. If your Beagle is overweight, work with your vet to set up a weight-management plan for your Beagle.

CHAPTER 15
Grooming Your Beagle

"Beagles do shed a lot. They have quite thick coats with an abundance of undercoat that sheds year round. This undercoat is perfect for making dust bunnies. Beagles also have a top coat with longer hairs that you'll find on your clothes and furniture."

Cindy Williams
Honey Pot Hounds

Grooming your Beagle is an important aspect of keeping your Beagle healthy and looking his best. From brushing and bathing your Beagle to cleaning his teeth and ears, Beagles take a bit of upkeep that will become easier to work into your daily life as you continue to groom your Beagle throughout his life.

Coat Basics

Your Beagle's coat is soft and shiny, and probably one of your favorite pastimes may be petting your pooch, so making sure your Beagle's skin and coat stay beautiful and healthy should be on your to-do list. A healthy coat should look shiny and feel smooth to the touch. A Beagle's coat is dense enough to be waterproof, but only medium-length, so caring for his coat should be relatively easy compared to caring for the coats of longhaired dogs. Keep in mind, though, that your Beagle's coat still requires regular grooming and upkeep to keep it looking and feeling healthy.

A dull coat can indicate a lot of things and doesn't necessarily reflect badly on you as a pet parent. Your dog may have a skin condition, and a dull coat can be a first indication. If you notice that your Beagle's coat is dull, pay attention to see if your dog is scratching more than usual or is shedding more than usual. If you find this to be the case, speak to your veterinarian about further steps.

HELPFUL TIP
Ear Cleaning and Health

The nature of a Beagle's ears may lead to infections that can reoccur. Vigilant cleaning and regular ear care will prove helpful in maintaining well-being. Use all of your senses when checking your dog's ears. Look inside for dirt, scrapes, and any discharge. Your own nose should help you "sniff out" when trouble may be brewing, as well. The odor from a dog's ear is unpleasant when infected. Use mineral oil on a cotton ball to gently wipe out the ears. Do not use a cotton swab or go any deeper than your first knuckle while cleaning. Avoid using rubbing alcohol to clean ears because it can be too drying. If you see a discharge that won't clear up, take your dog to the vet for professional care.

If your pup doesn't have a skin condition and you start to notice his coat is dull, it's likely because of an unbalanced diet that isn't providing the proper nutrients your dog needs. Diets low in fat can led to a rough, dry coat, and some grains can cause skin problems in dogs. Essential fatty acids are what keep your Beagle's coat looking shiny and healthy.

Dry skin is another cause of a dull coat. Some dogs just naturally have dry skin or may have dry skin because of the environment you live in. Using a shampoo designed to moisturize your dog's coat can help where your dog's diet and environment can't.

When to Bathe Your Beagle

*Photo Courtesy of
Donna Wells*

Bathing your Beagle, in general, contributes to how his coat looks. With the exception of your dog getting into something he shouldn't, Beagles do not require more than two to three baths a year. Bathing more often will cause your Beagle's coat to dry out as it loses the healthy oils that naturally build up on his skin and coat. Times when your dog is shedding are best for baths, typically spring and fall.

How to Bathe Your Beagle

Even though your Beagle will need only a few baths each year, the first year of your Beagle's life is more likely to be filled with several baths as your Beagle puppy discovers what actions can lead to a bath.

Puppies from a pet store are used to being in cages with other puppies and will poop wherever there is room because they haven't been trained otherwise. As such, those puppies will walk in waste during playtime or when trying to attract attention. Your Beagle may do the same in-

CHAPTER 15   Grooming Your Beagle

side of his kennel or anywhere in your home, tracking poop throughout the house and requiring bathing.

Regardless of whether your dog has tracked unpleasant mess through your home or has just discovered mud for the first time, your Beagle pup will likely have his first bath shortly after you bring him home, and you should know how to quickly and calmly bathe your dog.

1. Choose a place to bathe your Beagle. This can be the bathtub, the sink, or outside, depending on the size of your Beagle and your preference.

2. Gather all the supplies you'll need to bathe your Beagle including a coat-moisturizing shampoo, a brush, and a towel. A leash and a collar are optional, but remember that a wet dog may roll in anything to get the water and smell of soap off him.

3. Spend a few minutes brushing out the excess fur and dirt that may be on your dog's coat. Doing so will allow the shampoo to work better both at getting your dog clean as well as at keep his skin and coat healthy.

4. In your chosen bath area, completely wet your Beagle using a gentle setting on your water hose, kitchen sprayer, or showerhead. Do not wet his head at this step—you will clean that last. Start with wetting his neck and work your way down his body.

5. Apply the moisturizing shampoo generously to his coat, massaging the suds evenly into his skin. I generally just use my hands, but you may buy a bathing scrub for your Beagle's bath time.

6. Clean your Beagle's neck, back, tail, stomach, paws, and between his toes. Be gentle with his feet.

7. Using your hands and a small amount of shampoo, gently clean the top of your dog's head and back. Be careful around his ears, eyes, mouth, and nose. Consider using a washcloth and water to clean these areas to avoid getting shampoo in a sensitive place. A washcloth can also clean the shampoo from these areas instead of rinsing it away.

8. Starting from the neck again, rinse your Beagle well as leftover shampoo may dry out his coat. After he is thoroughly rinsed, use a towel to dry him and keep him inside until he's completely dry.

Be careful about getting water inside of your Beagle's ears. Consider gently placing cotton balls inside of his ears before you begin bathing him, or buy a dog accessory specifically designed to go over your dog's ears during bath time. If your Beagle hates baths, consider bath accessories that distract your dog during bath time with treats to keep him calm

and make the whole process easier. If your dog isn't heavily soiled, consider a shampoo-less bath to keep more of his natural oils present on his skin and fur.

If this is your Beagle's first bath, the process may not be as simple as described above. Dogs don't enjoy the same smells we do, so he may not like the smell of the shampoo you use, will probably struggle to get away from the water you pour over him, and may overall just be uncooperative.

Try acclimating your puppy to the bathing area slowly before he actually needs a bath. Use treats to get him to willingly come to the bathroom. You may even try getting him used to standing in water over the course of a few days and weeks by slightly increasing the level of water in your tub and placing your Beagle inside. Reward him for being in the water comfortably and calmly or for playing in the water. Allow your Beagle time to make positive associations with bathing.

Why Trim Your Beagle's Nails

"Keep their toe nails trimmed regularly, and clean their teeth often. Teeth cleaning chews can be a big help."

Gregg Moore
Moore Beagles

I have to admit, trimming Arthur's nails is the scariest thing for me even though I'm used to trimming his nails, other dogs' nails, and cats' nails. It's just always a worry as Arthur doesn't enjoy the process and without proper care, the opportunity for pain is likely. For the comfort of both you and your Beagle, start trimming early in your dog's life so both of you are used to it and learn what to expect.

First, let's talk about why you should be regularly trimming your Beagle's nails as well as what happens when you allow the nails to become overgrown.

Trimming your dog's nails is vital to keeping them healthy and is your responsibility not only as your Beagle's owner but also because humans, over the years, have changed the living environment of dogs to the point that their nails no longer naturally wear down by themselves. Nails that grow too long can become frail and break easily while your dog is running or playing, causing pain during the fracture or when the ragged edges get snagged on something.

A dog's nails grow continuously throughout his life, just like a human's nails. Unlike a human's nails, though, inside of a dog's nail is what's called a quick, a blood vessel and a nerve that can bleed and cause pain if cut.

The quick will grow down through the dog's nail if the nail is left untrimmed, and at that point, it may be impossible to avoid causing your dog pain. In that case, you should take your dog to a veterinarian to help with trimming. A vet will trim a dog's nails slowly, over time, to allow the quick to recede, avoiding pain for your pup altogether but also giving you a hefty vet bill for the trouble.

Ensuring that you regularly trim your Beagle's nails will prevent the quick from growing too far in the first place. Cutting the quick may happen, even if you are experienced at cutting your dog's nails, so make sure you have styptic powder on hand in case you need to stanch the bleeding. Cutting the quick is not life-threatening, just painful.

Photo Courtesy of Sheila Villegas

Overgrown nails can also affect the way your dog walks and cause him to experience a lot of pain as his skeletal structure is changed. Overgrown nails can lead to ingrown nails that can become infected.

A Beagle will need its nails trimmed once every one to two weeks. If you hear the clickity-clack of your dog's nails on your floors when he's walking, it's time for a nail trim. If you've got carpeted floors, you can decide visually if your Beagle's nails are too long. The claw shouldn't reach over the flesh pad of your dog's toes and also should not touch the ground when your Beagle is standing

How to Trim Your Beagle's Nails

To begin trimming your dog's nails, you first need to know which tool you will use. There are two common trimming tools: the nail clipper and the nail grinder.

The nail clipper comes in two different types: the scissor-type and the guillotine-type. Which you choose depends on your own hand or wrist pain as well as the thickness of your dog's nails. The guillotine-type takes less force and will be easier on the user's hands. The scissor-type is stronger and recommended for larger dogs. Since Beagles are small-to-medium-sized dogs, either choice is fine. Nail clippers will be faster than grinding but require that you be exact in where you make the cut on your dog's nails, to avoid the quick.

The nail grinder is electric and results in a smooth, rounded nail that doesn't leave a jagged edge to get caught on fabric or scratch humans. The nail grinder is a good option for dogs who have been traumatized by nail clippers and distrust them. It's still possible to hit the quick with grinding, but since the process is slower, you have much more control over avoiding the quick than you do with clippers. It may also be easier to see the quick when using a grinder unless your dog's nails are black or another dark color that makes it hard to see.

You may need to experiment with these tools to see which works best for you and your Beagle. Grinders can make a noise that scares dogs, but your dog may get used to the noise with time. Clippers may make you feel afraid of hurting your pup, but they make the process go by much faster.

Trimming With Clippers

1. Gently and steadily hold your dog's paw in your hand. This step is one you should get your dog used to way before you need to trim his nails. As always, use treats and praise to reward your Beagle for letting you hold his paw and to associate the act with happy things.

2. Even with treats, your dog may be cautious about the mysterious tool you're putting close to him. Let him sniff the clippers and get used to you holding them.

3. With either the guillotine or scissor clippers, insert the tip of your dog's nail between the blades. Starting with a very small portion will help you avoid the quick, especially if the quick isn't easy to see beneath your dog's nails.

4. Clip the small portion of your dog's nail, then give him a treat. He'll soon learn the process isn't one to fear. File down any rough edges left behind.

5. If you cut the quick, use styptic powder (or cornstarch) to stop the bleeding. It will probably bleed a lot, but besides the pain your dog will not forget, there is no lasting physical harm. Use a damp wash-

cloth to clean away the blood and styptic powder once the bleeding has stopped.

Trimming With a Grinder

1. Gently and steadily hold your dog's paw in your hand. This step is one you should get your dog used to way before you need to trim his nails. As always, use treats and praise to reward your Beagle for letting you hold his paw and to associate the act with happy things.

2. Even with treats, your dog may be cautious about the mysterious tool you're putting close to him. Let him sniff the grinder and get used to you holding it.

Photo Courtesy of Casey Murdough

3. Tap the nail and grinder together for no more than three seconds at a time, being careful not to leave it there for long. You may grind too far down or cause heat friction on the nail.

4. Be sure that the grinder is turning outward from your dog's paw; otherwise, the grinder may push the nail back uncomfortably.

5. If you happen to hit the quick, use styptic powder (or cornstarch) to stop the bleeding. It will probably bleed a lot, but besides the pain your dog will not forget, there is no lasting physical harm. Use a damp washcloth to clean away the blood and styptic powder once the bleeding has stopped.

Don't worry about trimming the nail too short. The quick will recede as you habitually trim the nails, and cutting or grinding the nails will be easier and less stressful with time as you and your Beagle get used to the process.

Overall, there are many reasons you should be trimming your dog's nails as well as easy-to-use tools for getting the job done. The process isn't difficult with practice, but if you're not comfortable trimming nails, there are other options.

One option is to walk or play with your dog on a rough surface such as asphalt or concrete. These rough surfaces will help wear your Beagle's nails down. If you have a concrete patio in your backyard, encourage your Beagle to play in this area.

Go jogging together on asphalt often; this will provide you and your Beagle with some exercise as well as wearing down his nails. Agility practice is another source of exercise that can naturally wear down your Beagle's nails, and Beagles are already know for their agility. Some agility equipment has a sandpaper-like texture that will help file down your Beagle's nails.

Another option is one I sometimes use. An emery board or nail file can work well, though slowly if your dog doesn't like nail clippers or grinders. I got Arthur used to me touching his paws and toes using this method as he was overly cautious about me handling his paws.

These alternative options may work for some, but Beagle nails grow quickly, so you may need to go with one of the usual nail-trimming options or hire a professional to do the trimming if these alternatives don't work.

Dental Care

There are two really easy and simple ways to keep your Beagle's teeth healthy.

Dental snacks are the first, and easiest way. Dental snacks come hard, soft, chewy, and everything in between and are designed to improve your dog's bad breath and to prevent a buildup of bacteria and tartar. Dental snacks are a really easy method of keeping your Beagle's teeth clean because he'll love being given a snack, to begin with, and won't even consider that it's actually helping him. Dental snacks are a must to help control bad doggy breath.

While dental snacks are great, brushing your dog's teeth is the most effective way to keep his teeth healthy, but dogs hate having people messing around with their mouths, so it will take some training and acclimating to get your dog comfortably used to having his teeth brushed.

First, as with every new situation you introduce your Beagle to, spend some time getting him used to you putting things in his mouth. On a daily basis, allow him to lick a bit of peanut butter off of your finger. Touch his teeth to get him used to the act, and praise him for letting you do so. Graduate to toothpaste made specifically for dogs (do not use human toothpaste on your dog), then begin introducing him to the toothbrush by letting him sniff and examine it. Continue to praise him.

Once you've got him licking toothpaste off the brush, then you can start getting him used to having his teeth brushed. Start off with short sessions of brushing his teeth. You don't need to get all his teeth at once, and you will allow him to get used to the process if you go slowly.

As your Beagle gets acclimated to the process, you can spend more time brushing his teeth and even get to areas he wouldn't allow you to brush at first.

If your Beagle has gone a while without having his teeth cleaned, he may require a professional dental cleaning to remove plaque and tartar buildup. Pets can also develop periodontal disease just like humans, a disease that infects the structures around the teeth. The infection can spread if left untreated.

Signs of periodontal disease included swollen or red gums, bad breath, and bleeding gums.

Cleaning Beagle Ears

Your Beagle's ears are one of his most obvious features, floppy and long and working to help him catch more new and interesting scents as he waves his ears around in the air.

A Beagle's ears need to be cleaned regularly, at least once a week, as Beagles are prone to ear problems such as waxy buildup or infections.

Cleaning your Beagle ears is pretty simple! All you need are cotton balls, which are the perfect size to keep you from going too deep into your dog's ear and possibly causing damage. Do not use Q-Tips to clean your Beagle's ears.

If your dog's ears do get infected, have a bad smell, or seem to be bothering her, speak to your veterinarian about treatments. They will likely give you an ear-cleaning solution to help with the problem.

Cleaning Beagle Eyes

You've probably noticed how some dogs have eye discharge or eye boogers, even when they haven't just woken up (like in humans). Beagles have a lot of eye discharge, and if left uncleaned, it can build up and attract dust and grime that can get into your dog's eyes.

Eye discharge can be clear and watery, gooey, or crusty. This gunk isn't usually serious and can be wiped away with a damp cloth. No soap is necessary and, in fact, you should keep soap away from your dog's eyes. It isn't recommended that you use your fingers to clean this gunk, but as long as your hands are clean and you're not directly touching your dog's eye, using your fingers should cause your Beagle no harm, and since Beagles produce a LOT of eye gunk, you'll go through a lot of damp cloths cleaning it.

There are additional products you can buy to clean your Beagle's ears such as baby wipes, eye drops, eye washes, tearstain remover (if the gunk is staining your dog's fur), and eye combs. Most of these tools aren't necessary for day-to-day gunk cleaning.

Signs that the eye gunk is something more to be worried about is if the gunk has a pus-like consistency, is a white-gray mucus, is yellow or green, or if your Beagle has unusually red eyes. These symptoms could indicate an immune condition, eye infection, or other medical problem, and if you notice these symptoms, you should consult your veterinarian immediately.

147

CHAPTER 16
Basic Health Care

Visiting the Vet

The health of your Beagle is probably your top priority, and as such, you probably have a lot of questions that are best answered by a qualified professional. You should have an idea of which veterinarian you want to take your Beagle to before you bring her home. Depending on the age of your Beagle, she may still need to go get her vaccines, which means a trip to the vet every three to five weeks until 16 weeks of age, but most dogs should have passed the age for these early vaccinations by the time they come home with you.

Even if your pup is past this age and already has all of her vaccinations, you want to take her to the vet shortly after you bring her home not only so you can get a second opinion about her health, but also in order to establish her with her new vet.

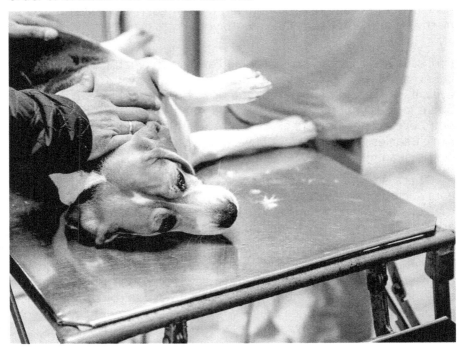

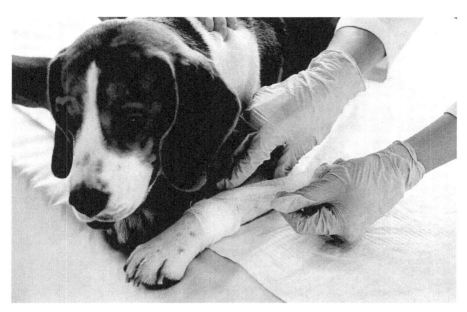

After the initial vet visits, it's recommended that you take your dog in to see the vet at least once a year for a checkup. Your vet will give your dog a physical, do bloodwork, take a fecal sample, and just overall ensure your Beagle is in tiptop shape.

If your vet does find any problems with your pup, they may order more tests or send you to another facility that is better equipped to treat your Beagle.

There are other reasons you may need to visit the vet outside of your Beagle's yearly checkup. One of the most common reasons for visiting the vet is to test for and get treatment for fleas, ticks, worms, and other harmful parasites that may have migrated onto or into your Beagle's body.

Fleas and Ticks

Fleas and ticks are the most common pests that pet owners encounter. Fleas and ticks can live in your dog's fur and feed on your dog's blood, often causing allergic reactions on your dog's skin and spreading illnesses. These pests are more common during warm months, but in some areas, fleas and ticks are a year-round bother.

The most obvious sign of fleas is constant scratching. Your dog may excessively lick or scratch herself if she has fleas as she tries to soothe

Photo Courtesy of
Bill Arsham

the irritated bites they leave. If your Beagle has fleas, not only will you notice her scratching but you may also suffer from mysterious and painful itches yourself. You may not have any comfy fur for fleas to hide in, but they still want to (and will) drink your blood. If you notice bumps or itchy skin on your feet, ankles, or legs, you may have fleas and may need to treat your whole house as well as your pup to get rid of them.

Another indication of fleas is black and white specks either on your Beagle's fur or in his favorite sleeping areas. The black specks are flea droppings, and when wet, they will turn a reddish-brown color (because of the blood). The white specks are flea eggs, and if you've noticed the white specks, you may be horrified at how many of them there are dropping from your Beagle's fur. Fleas can lay 40-50 eggs in a single day, so start early to prevent fleas before you have to treat your home for them. Sources of fleas include other animals who may be infected, grass, patios, and infected furniture.

Ticks are bigger than fleas, so you may notice signs of them sooner. Ticks like to attach themselves on the head, near the ears, and on the neck. If you feel a bump on your dog while petting him, it may be a tick. Ticks can carry dangerous diseases and spread them not only to your dog but also to your family.

Ticks can survive a year without feeding, and they hide in grass or on bushes, waiting for a suitable host to pass by and attach to. Cold months are usually free of ticks, but wooded areas, warm areas, and areas in the northeast are more likely to have ticks in general.

Signs of ticks include loss of appetite, fever, swollen joints, and swollen lymph nodes. Ticks can pass on Lyme disease and even cause severe muscle weakness in your dog along with other serious illnesses. Ticks should be treated as soon as there are signs.

Dogs that lose too much blood because of fleas or ticks can develop anemia. Signs of anemia in dogs include pale gums and a lack of energy. Some dogs may develop skin rashes because of an allergic reaction to flea saliva.

Your veterinarian can help you treat your Beagle for both fleas and ticks, although there are at-home treatments for both that usually work fine.

Flea and tick collars are a popular choice for preventing infection and even treating an infection (though I wouldn't rely solely on them for treatment). These collars usually last a long time before needing to be replaced, but some animals develop a sensitivity on the skin around their necks. Not every pet will be affected by a collar, even if another animal has suffered from a specific brand. If you use a flea collar and notice loss of fur, red skin, or a rash around your dog's neck, remove the collar and

Photo Courtesy of Scott Pendlebury

Photo Courtesy of
Abby Myers

discontinue use. Gently clean the area with a damp cloth. Medical treatment may be needed if your dog is sick beyond the skin rash.

Flea and tick shampoos are a more common and more affordable treatment, but they don't prevent fleas, and you may also leave fleas and ticks behind if you don't clean your dog's fur thoroughly enough. People usually rinse their dogs too soon when giving flea and tick baths. Wait at least 10 minutes before rinsing your dog's fur to ensure all the current pests are dead.

Flea and tick pills are another option, though they can be expensive, and convincing your dog to take a pill may be hard. Fortunately, you can easily hide one of these pills in your Beagle's food, and she'll gobble it up too quickly to notice that you've medicated her. You can get flea and tick pills from your veterinarian.

Probably the most common treatment for fleas and ticks is the topical skin treatment. Once a month, you'll apply a premeasured amount of this treatment to your dog's back, between her shoulder blades. Depending on the product, this treatment may kill fleas and ticks as well as their eggs, or just fleas and ticks. You can buy this product in stores, but it's recommended that you speak with a veterinarian about the right treatment for you.

A flea and tick comb is another option if you want to avoid chemical pesticides, but they require a lot of work and attention to detail, and you may miss some pests if not careful. Combs will help get rid of fleas, their eggs, and their droppings.

There are some holistic and natural alternatives that people often want to try for their dogs. Some of them may work, but others are dangerous for your dog as some of these natural remedies can cause severe reactions to your dog or her skin. These include geranium, eucalyptus oil, pennyroyal oil, garlic, and onions. It's wise to consult your veterinarian before giving your Beagle a natural or alternative treatment.

Natural remedies aren't all bad, though, as long as you're using the right product. Your dog may need a natural product for her sensitive skin, or you may need it for yourself if the pesticide you've been using causes a negative reaction. Dogs who don't go outside much also will benefit from alternative remedies as some of these treatments are pre-treatments for when you know your dog may be exposed to fleas or ticks.

To prevent fleas and ticks in your home, consider treating your yard to eliminate these pests before they have a chance to attach themselves to your dog and enter your home.

Worms

Worms are truly disgusting, and you definitely don't want them infecting your dog and, possibly, the rest of your family. There are a few common types of worms dogs can be infected with, and they can cause trouble throughout your dog's body as they travel and invade different areas.

Heartworms

Photo Courtesy of Monika Barany

Heartworms can lead to congestive heart failure in dogs. Heartworms are thin worms that can multiply and grow up to 12 inches in your dog's heart. Your vet should check for heartworms during your Beagle's checkup. Prevention is key because heartworms are carried by mosquitoes, a common and hard-to-kill pest.

Depending on the severity of the infection, signs of heartworms may include an intolerance for exercise, a mild cough, loss of appetite, weight loss, and lethargy.

Roundworms

Roundworms are one of the most common worms dogs will be infected with. They live in the intestines of dogs and can be transmitted to people. Humans can be infected directly by feces or by dirt where an infected dog has defecated. Dogs can be infected by their environment, through contact with another animal's feces, and even by their mother's milk at a very young age. Reinfection is common, so good hygiene concerning your dog is important. This is also why flushing your dog's poop is discouraged as worms and eggs are known to survive sewage treatment.

Infection isn't easy to notice, but in some cases, signs of roundworm include coughing, vomiting, lethargy, abnormal feces, and anorexia.

Tapeworms

Tapeworms are another common intestinal worm that can also be transmitted to humans. Signs of tapeworm include butt scooting and licking as your dog attempts to relieve the itchiness caused by the worms. Tapeworm egg casings also drop from your dog's anus, so you may see signs of them stuck on the outside of his fur, in his favorite sleeping areas, or on the floor. These egg casings are small and white, and when they dry up, they look like tiny grains of rice. When these casings are fresh, they may wriggle around, dropping thousands of impossible-to-see eggs.

Hookworms

Hookworms feed on your dog's blood via the intestines and can lead to anemia, especially in young dogs. Signs of infection include weight loss or inability to gain weight, bloody or black stool, weakness, pale gums, diarrhea, and coughing.

Whipworms

Adult female whipworms can survive for months or years in your dog's intestines, producing 1000-4000 eggs a day. Whipworms are most common in dogs compared to other animals, though they don't usually cause problems as severe as other worms. Signs of infection include bloody stool, watery stool, weight loss, dehydration, weakness, and anemia.

Ringworms

While not actually a worm, this fungus can grow and live on the skin and hair follicles, and even nails of your dog. Ringworm is highly contagious and can quickly spread all over your dog as well as to the rest of your family. Ringworm is spread by touch, so simply petting or scratching your dog can put you at risk for infection.

Ringworm is not serious and is easily treatable, but it can definitely cause discomfort for anyone infected with it. Keeping your dog's bedding and favorite sleeping areas clean can help prevent the spread of ringworm, and you can find an oral or topical treatment either at your local pet store or prescribed by your vet.

Identifying which worms your dog is infected with may be tricky, so at the first signs of infection, you should take your Beagle to the vet immediately. Your vet can identify the type of parasite infecting your dog and prescribe the appropriate treatment.

Holistic Alternatives

Holistic alternatives and dietary supplements are more and more popular for treating beloved pets, but it's important to consult a licensed veterinarian before proceeding with any such treatment, and you should let a professional actually perform these treatments.

Acupuncture and acupressure are both based on traditional Chinese medicine and can treat muscular injuries and anxiety. This treatment also helps to correct the balance of blood flow to help the body heal itself. This treatment is noninvasive and gentle. Only a trained acupuncturist should apply treatment to your dog.

QUOTE

Holistic Approaches to Pet Care

According to the American Kennel Club website (akc.org), Americans "spend $30 billion annually on alternative and holistic treatments." Included in that amount is pet care. The American Holistic Veterinary Medical Association (ahvma.org) is a resource for conventional and complementary care for your pet. The website includes information on holistic therapies such as acupuncture, massage, water therapy, and sound therapy. Check for recommendations on their site for holistic veterinarians in your area.

Chiropractic treatment is a much gentler procedure for dogs than it is for humans and can help dogs with back problems. A trained veterinary chiropractor can help dogs who suffer from pain or loss of agility by manipulating and realigning the spine and other bones. This treatment can also relieve joint or muscular pain.

Massages can calm anxious dogs, relieve muscular tension, and improve blood flow in your dog's body. Some experts even think that massages can improve the immune and digestive systems, aid the removal of toxins, and decrease blood pressure. There are trained animal massage therapists, but this treatment is one you can learn to do yourself, and your dog will definitely enjoy getting a massage at home whenever you're in the mood to spoil him.

Some owners choose to supplement their dogs' diets with vitamins such as glucosamine, omega-3 fatty acids, probiotics, or another type of vitamin or multivitamin. While some dogs need these supplements, not all dogs do. Consult your veterinarian before adding vitamins to your dog's diet as too much of even a good thing can be harmful.

Vaccinations

Your veterinarian will let you know when it's time to vaccinate your Beagle. Keep a record of your dog's last vaccinations in case you have to switch vets. Avoid vaccinating during times of illness or stress such as during pregnancy, before travel, when in a new living environment, or around the time of another preventive treatment unless otherwise approved by your vet. Your Beagle should have all necessary vaccinations by 16 weeks of age. After this time, boosters and rabies shots may be the only vaccinations needed.

Some dogs may develop a negative reaction to vaccines which can include swelling, trouble breathing, lethargy, vomiting, diarrhea, hives, or a drooping eye. These signs often don't manifest until some hours after the vaccination, so keep an eye on your pup for about six hours after vaccinating. If you do notice any of these symptoms, seek treatment immediately.

Pet Insurance

Medical treatment is expensive whether it's for a human or for an animal, and when something unexpected happens to your four-legged loved one, you want to know that you'll not only be able to take your pet to the vet at any time but also that you'll be able to cover the cost of treatment, which, depending on the diagnosis, can be thousands of dollars.

Pet insurance or pet health plans work the same as a human's health plan by helping cover the cost of medical care in case of illness or injury. Some plans also cover your dog's annual vaccinations, vet visits, and testing. Be aware that not all pet health-care plans are pet insurance. Some don't cover accidents or emergency care but just pay for vet office visits or annual treatments.

When searching for and choosing pet insurance, look for a plan that covers a wide range of treatments and services such as emergency care, cancer, hereditary conditions, alternative treatments, blood tests and body scans, surgery, and anything else you can think of. No one insurance plan will cover it all, so look for the specific coverage that works best for you and your Beagle.

CHAPTER 17
Advanced Beagle Health and Aging Dog Care

Common Diseases and Conditions in Beagles

Beagles are a mostly healthy breed, but some conditions and diseases may present themselves during your dog's life that you want to prepare yourself for.

Glaucoma is a common condition that Beagles suffer from. If untreated, canine glaucoma can lead to blindness as a result of pressure from the stretching of the eye. The stretching is caused by an excess of naturally occurring liquid that isn't adequately drained from the eye. Symptoms include different-sized pupils, blood vessels in the whites of the eyes, tearing, or swollen eyes.

Cherry eye occurs when the gland of a dog's third eyelid slips out of place, resulting in a red or pink sac that is visible in the corner of the dog's eye. The purpose of this gland is to produce tears, but this condition can lead to swelling of the gland and discomfort for your dog. The cause of this condition is unknown and can be corrected surgically.

Photo Courtesy of Sarah Hadley

*Photo Courtesy of
Scott Pendlebury*

Distichiasis is another eye condition Beagles can develop. This condition causes the eyelashes of a Beagle to grow abnormally and bend into the eyelid, causing irritation to the cornea. This condition isn't serious, but your Beagle may show his displeasure by pawing at his face. Treatment involves a vet trimming the eyelashes on a regular basis.

Diabetes is another condition Beagles share with humans. Just like in humans, type 1 diabetes is a genetic inheritance caused by an insufficient production of insulin. Beagles may also develop type 2 diabetes if they overeat and become overweight. Type 2 diabetes is preventable with proper diet and exercise. Symptoms include excessive thirst, lethargy, increased urination, and change in appetite. Canine diabetes can be managed with diet, exercise, and insulin injections.

Epilepsy is a neurological disorder resulting in sudden and uncontrolled seizing. An episode of epilepsy can be scary as your dog's limbs may twitch and jerk, and he may lose consciousness. This condition can be a result of genetics or consumption of caffeine. Epilepsy may cause permanent brain damage or lead to death.

Ear infections are common in Beagles because of their long and floppy ears. Many foreign objects can become trapped in your Beagle's ear, leading to an infection if left uncleaned. Symptoms of ear infection include a bad odor coming from the infected ear and head shaking. Early treatment can help prevent discomfort for your Beagle.

Another condition found in Beagles is chondrodystrophy or Beagle dwarfism. This condition can cause poor cartilage development and presents itself by shortening the legs and causing premature degeneration of

Photo Courtesy of
Philip Rhodes

a Beagle's intervertebral discs. Chondrodystrophy may take up to a year to present, and knowing the medical history of your Beagle's bloodline can help alert you to the possibility of this condition. This condition can cause your Beagle a lot of pain that may not be noticed for years and which can cause your Beagle difficulty with walking and holding up his head.

Hip dysplasia is a genetic condition many Beagles suffer from, and this condition can cause arthritis in dogs. This condition often doesn't present itself until later in life when the soft tissue around a Beagle's hips begins to develop abnormally. Beagles with hip dysplasia have trouble walking or running, and they may also lose function of their joins. Obesity can worsen this condition and the symptoms.

Hypothyroidism is caused by an autoimmune disorder that causes your dog's body to think something harmful is in your dog's thyroid, resulting in the body attacking the gland. This condition isn't life threatening and can be managed over the course of your Beagle's life. Symptoms include a dull coat, lethargy, weight gain, and hair loss.

Illness and Injury Prevention

While many conditions and inherited traits are outside of your control, there are some illnesses and injuries you can ensure your dog avoids.

Dogs can become injured in fights with other animals, by falling from too high, in a car accident, by running into things, or by overexerting themselves. You can prevent these injuries by keeping a close eye on your Beagle while around other dogs, eliminating access to high places in your home, keeping your Beagle on a leash while out, and by ensuring your Beagle doesn't work too hard when doing exercises or agility training.

Other injuries include oral injuries as a result of chewing on bones or other inappropriately-hard or sharp objects, resulting in torn or bleeding gums, tongue, and teeth. Keep such objects out of reach of your Beagle, and train him to drop something when you command him to.

A Beagle may also tear his toenails or get cuts and scratches while playing. These injuries can occur because of the surfaces your dog plays on or the environment in which he plays. If your dog has many cuts and scratches, it may be because of rough foliage or branches on your property that you should cut back. Toenails can be caught on anything and be painfully torn. Preventing such injuries is as simple as keeping his nails trimmed and watching where he plays.

All dogs have the possibility of having their tails injured either because they've whacked them against something much too hard or because they've gotten caught in a closing door or under a heavy foot. Depending on the severity of the injury, treatment can be difficult and take time.

HELPFUL TIP
Your Aging Dog

Your dog's coat is starting to become gray; he is slowing down and is not as spry as he once was. These signs of aging are only external signs; many other age-related conditions may be hiding inside your aging dog. Dogs suffer from many conditions that plague humans as they reach the "golden years." Gastrointestinal problems may surface as he enters the senior stage of his life. Excess weight should be monitored and managed because it may bring along many unwanted conditions in your pet. Your overweight dog may have difficulty breathing and can be prone to heart disease, diabetes, high blood pressure, arthritis, and cancer. Be diligent with your dog's nutrition and exercise needs at this stage of his life. You are your pet's greatest advocate.

Basics of Senior Dog Care

Beagles are expected to live between 13 and 15 years and are considered to be senior dogs at nine years of age at which time your Beagle should begin geriatric exams. Geriatric exams allow your vet to plan future care around your Beagle's elderly years.

During a geriatric exam, your vet should complete a more thorough examination than usual to look for abnormalities in your Beagle's ears, eyes, gums, organs, muscles, muscles, skin, and bones.

You should expect a few lifestyle changes as your Beagle ages. Her eating habits will surely change as she ages, and your Beagle should be switched to a dog food appropriate for her new life stage. If your Beagle develops any gum or tooth-related diseases, she may be more reluctant

Photo Courtesy of
Amanda BourQuard

to eat. Dog food can be softened to help with chewing, or you can switch to a wet dog food suitable for senior dogs.

Your Beagle's weight may fluctuate as she ages; she may gain more weight as her metabolism slows and walking becomes more difficult, or she may lose weight as eating becomes harder and her appetite wanes. She's also likely to sleep more often because of the decrease in activity. Senior Beagles will become tired faster while playing, so be aware of when your senior dog has had enough of playtime and let her rest. You should consider buying a pet bed made specifically for elderly dogs to improve the comfort of your Beagle's sleep.

Inactivity can also prevent your Beagle's nails from wearing down naturally, so you may have to increase trimming. The pads of your Beagle's paws may also become more sensitive as they thicken with age. A paw wax can help protect sensitive paws.

Even though your Beagle may be reluctant to exercise for various reasons, you should continue to provide her with exercise suitable for her age and health conditions to help her maintain her health. Obesity can make old age much harder and more painful for your Beagle than it needs to be.

Your senior Beagle may develop trouble holding her bladder because of weakened digestive muscles or another medical problem that comes with old age. You may need to increase trips outside, keep puppy training pads inside for easy access, or even invest in canine diapers.

As your Beagle ages, her hearing and eyesight may worsen, making responding to verbal or visual commands more difficult or altogether impossible. At the same time, your Beagle may have a lot less energy to get into trouble. Your Beagle may become easily startled if she's unable to hear or see when people are approaching her. You and your family should approach your senior Beagle within her line of sight.

Grooming

As your Beagle ages, grooming will become more of a chore for her. She's more likely to experience discomfort and pain, so you should be considerate. Grooming oftentimes involves dogs standing for long periods of time or being in awkward positions. Your Beagle may become grumpy and just refuse to be groomed if you don't take care.

Elderly Beagles require grooming more often than younger Beagles. You should clean her ears every day, bathe her weekly or biweekly, and clean her teeth more regularly. Nails are more likely to be brittle with old

Photo Courtesy of
Allie Muisenga

age, so take care with trimming, and keep nails short to avoid a painful-ly-broken nail.

When brushing your Beagle, make sure the brush's bristles aren't rough or split as your Beagle's skin is more sensitive at this stage of her life. Be gentle with brushing, and consider giving her a massage before or after the brushing. Move slowly to avoid startling your Beagle.

When bathing your Beagle, pay more attention to areas your dog is used to cleaning herself as old age may make reaching these areas more difficult. Consider trimming around these areas to keep them clean. Also use a nonslip mat to secure your dog's footing wherever you bathe her. Keep the water warm, but not too hot for your elderly Beagle's sensitive skin.

Overall, keep grooming short; consider breaking up regular groom-ing throughout the week. For instance, you can trim her nails one day and brush her the next, so she doesn't become overwhelmed and overtired with the process. If you take your Beagle to a groomer to be groomed, make sure the groomer is taking the proper care for an elderly dog.

Nutrition

Nutrition becomes even more important as your Beagle ages. Just like there are special foods for puppies, there are also special foods for senior dogs that address the unique nutritional needs that come with old age.

Senior dogs will require fewer calories to prevent obesity and more protein as protein stores are depleted more quickly in older dogs. Dogs can lose muscle mass as they age without the proper amount of protein.

Depending on your Beagle's weight, you may need to reduce or increase her fat intake to balance her weight. Your veterinarian can tell you whether your Beagle is within a healthy weight range and what to do if she isn't.

Fiber becomes more important as anyone ages, and your senior Beagle may become constipated easily without proper fiber intake. Some senior dog foods have less fiber, to account for vitamin absorption, so speak with your vet about fiber supplements or alternatives to prevent constipation if needed.

Other dietary supplements may help you meet your elderly Beagle's nutritional needs, but you should consult your veterinarian before beginning a supplement treatment. Your veterinarian should also be consulted if there are changes in your Beagle's appetite.

Exercise

Exercise becomes more difficult with age but also more important as your dog's metabolism slows down. Some conditions an older dog may develop can make exercise more difficult and limit mobility in general. Having a plan to keep your elderly Beagle active may help with joint pain and weight gain.

Regular walks are a good exercise for senior dogs as is inside play with interactive toys. Don't allow your Beagle to overexert herself out of excitement during walks or playtime. Keep walks short, and watch for pain or discomfort during walks. Swimming is an alternative activity that elderly dogs may enjoy because the impact is low on the joints.

Overall, be patient with your senior dog. Realize that she's not as young as she used to be and that she may be experiencing pain during activities she used to effortlessly enjoy.

Common Old-age Ailments

Some ailments are common in dogs, no matter the breed.

One of the most common old-age ailments for dogs is dental disease. Dental disease can lead to pain, tooth loss, and organ-damaging bacteria in the bloodstream. Dogs can develop gingivitis or periodontal disease with age and improper dental care.

Dogs are commonly diagnosed with various cancers as they age including melanoma, bone cancer, and lymphoma. Early detection can help your Beagle survive cancer, and your vet can test for cancers during visits.

Osteoarthritis and joint pain are natural as one ages, and dogs are not exempt from this fact. As dogs age, the cartilage protecting their joints degrades, causing pain in these areas.

Dementia is, sadly, another ailment elder dogs may experience. This ailment may result in personality changes, disorientation, and general confusion.

When It's Time to Say Goodbye

Saying goodbye to a beloved family member can be difficult, especially when it seems like you just brought her home yesterday. Knowing and accepting when it's time is another pain altogether, but your veterinarian can help you by advising you on when euthanization is necessary.

If your dog is no longer enjoying life because of chronic pain that can't be controlled with medication, extreme weight loss coupled with vomiting or diarrhea, or complete loss of appetite, it may be time to say goodbye.

It can be hard to really accept that your Beagle is ready to move on, and you may want to keep fighting to keep her alive, but if your Beagle can't eat without you forcing her, is incontinent, and is no longer enjoying the toys and activities she used to, she isn't living the best life she could be.

While it is indeed hard to let go, you aren't letting go of the memories and love you have for your Beagle; you're freeing her from experiencing undo pain.

Once you've made the decision to say goodbye to your Beagle, your veterinarian will explain the euthanization process to you to help relieve stress on your part. Even though your vet will explain the procedure, feel free to ask any questions you need in order to understand and come to terms with the process.

While you may be present for the procedure, you may not be allowed to hold your pet during the process, but after your veterinarian has confirmed that your Beagle has passed, you will be allowed a few minutes alone.

You may choose to have your beloved Beagle cremated, and your vet may have options for the service. Burial is another option, either in your own back yard or in a pet cemetery.

Whichever option you choose, you will always have the memories of your Beagle. Though she may be gone, the happiness and joy she brought to your life is not. However you choose to remember your loved one, know that you both equally improved each other's life just by being together.

Photo Courtesy of
Kristin Smith

Made in the USA
Coppell, TX
24 May 2020

26369894R00095